AMBIGRAMS

REVEALED

NIKITA PROKHOROV

Ambigrams Revealed: A Graphic Designer's Guide to Creating Typographic Art Using Optical Illusions, Symmetry, and Visual Perception

Nikita Prokhorov

New Riders
www.newriders.com

To report errors, please send a note to errata@peachpit.com

New Riders is an imprint of Peachpit, a division of Pearson Education.

Acquisitions Editor: Nikki McDonald
Project Editor: Rebecca Gulick
Development and Copy Editor: Anne Marie Walker
Production Editor: Katerina Malone
Cover Design: Bastian Pinnenberg and Nikita Prokhorov
Interior Design: Nikita Prokhorov
Proofreader: Patricia Pane
Book title ambigram: Nikita Prokhorov
Front-cover ambigrams: Alejandro Ayala, Dave Bailey, Cleber Faria, Javier Sanchez Galvan, Brett J. Gilbert, Nicholas Gilbert, Tiffany Harvey, Scott Kim, Charles Krausie, Andrey Kruglov, John Langdon, Robert Maitland, Niels Shoe Meulman, David Moser, Vineeth Nair, Lisa Nemetz, Robert Petrick, Bastian Pinnenberg, Nikita Prokhorov, Rammer Martínez Sánchez, Cheryl Savala, Martin Schmetzer, Mark Simonson
Back-cover ambigrams: Prajyot Damle, Daniel Dostal, Brett J. Gilbert, Nabil Harb, Mark Hunter, Homero Larrain, Seb Lester, Vineeth Nair, Awang Purba, Mark Simonson, Martijn Slegers, Krzysztof Sliwa, Jessica Southwick, Stefan Vasilev, Jan Zabransky

ISBN-13: 978-0-321-85547-3
ISBN-10: 0-321-85547-7

9 8 7 6 5 4 3 2 1
Printed and bound in the United States of America

To my mother, grandmother, and grandfather.
I could not have asked for a more wonderful family.

ACKNOWLEDGMENTS

To my amazing mother, grandmother, and grandfather, thank you from the bottom of my heart. Words can't adequately express enough gratitude for what you've given to me throughout my entire life.

I would like to thank the talented ambigram community, without which this book would not be possible. It has been a privilege to connect with every one of you and have you participate in *Ambigrams Revealed*. The process of getting to know you, and discovery of your work in person (and via email) helped shape the vision for this book.

A special thanks goes out to Mark Hunter for inviting me to curate Ambigram.com in 2009. This, although unbeknownst to me at the time, set the wheels in motion for this book.

A group that I cannot thank enough is the incredible judging panel assembled for this book. Without the writings and comments of these judges, this book would simply have been a gallery of ambigrams and nothing more:

• Thank you to Cheryl Savala for her belief in my work and the inspiration she provided on a daily basis with her words.

• Thank you to Stefan G. Bucher for his humor and insight, and telling me to suck it up when the going got tough (and for his referral to Peachpit!).

• Thank you to John Langdon and Scott Kim for their contribution to the ambigram world and for setting the ambigram bar very high.

• Thank you to Maggie Macnab, Jessica Hische, and Scot Morris for their unique perspective on the work in this book.

Ambigrams Revealed would not exist without Peachpit and its fantastic staff. Nikki McDonald made me the happiest ambigrammist alive when she told me Peachpit would publish the book. Rebecca Gulick helped keep this project running like a well-oiled machine. Charlene Will provided some much needed design criticism and feedback while the book was in the developmental stages. Anne Marie Walker made sure that the body copy didn't just read, but sang, and her patience for my antics never wore thin. Her copyediting made the words come alive. And to everyone else on the Peachpit team, including Katerina Malone, Patricia Pane, Valerie Witte, and everyone else, thank you for your hard work on this book. Designers can sometimes be difficult to work with, and I appreciate that you've put up with me for so long!

To my fellow designers, thank you for your support. Without your feedback, humor, and wit, my sanity would've escaped a long time ago. Thank you for keeping my head in the game, for your support, and for your words—brutally critical or helpful, serious or humorous—every bit was greatly appreciated.

To my friends, thank you for being there and for listening to my humor and puns. And if you can't read my ambigrams, don't worry; at times I can't read them either.

TABLE OF CONTENTS

INTRODUCTION

Great discoveries usually happen by accident, and my ambigram discovery was no exception. I was sitting in a bookstore with a randomly selected book, *Angels & Demons*, by Dan Brown when I stumbled upon my very first ambigram (*Figure I.1*). The rest of the book ceased to exist as the next hour was spent with pencil and paper in hand in an attempt to figure out just how this typographic design worked. Although that attempt was not successful, giving up was not in my nature: I spent weeks researching and sketching before I created my first ambigram (*Figure I.2*). As raw as it was aesthetically, it was an ambigram: fairly legible, readable, and when rotated 180 degrees, it read the same. I was ecstatic, knowing that I had found a new artistic addiction that would not end with just one ambigram.

Figure I.1 Book title for *Angels & Demons*. (John Langdon)

Figure I.2 My first ambigram. (Nikita Prokhorov)

EXPLORING THE AMBIGRAM WORLD

The discovery of John Langdon and Scott Kim's work opened up a completely new world for me. My ambigram research led me to learn about fellow ambigram artists, such as NAGFA, Douglas Hofstadter, Bastian Pinnenberg, and many others. I decided to start an ambigram blog called Ambiblog to bring all the artists and knowledge together under one virtual roof. Shortly thereafter, Mark Hunter (the owner of ambigram.com) contacted me and asked if I wanted to write and design for ambigram.com. We began running monthly contests, conducting interviews, and posting ambigram-relevant content, trying to connect designers from every corner of the world. Ambigram.com became the largest and most popular online portal for ambigrammists, and I realized how international, diverse, and talented that community was.

WHAT'S IN AMBIGRAMS REVEALED?

Being connected to ambigram artists worldwide, it was only natural to consider the opportunity to showcase international talent that had never been published! Although artists like John Langdon, Scott Kim, and Douglas Hofstadter had published their individual work, a book featuring ambigrams from all over the world did not exist. The idea for *Ambigrams Revealed*

Figure I.3 Samples from the ambigram showcase. (From top to bottom: Cheryl Savala, Menagerie Creative; Scott Kim; and David Moser.)

was born—a book featuring several hundred unique ambigrams from around the world (*Figure I.3*), case studies that explored the process of ambigram design, and a panel of judges (experts in the ambigram and design fields) who would share their thoughts on ambigrams, as well as comment on the entries received. A "Call to Enter" was posted on ambigram.com, as well as on Facebook and other social media websites. Over 500 entries were submitted! The judges were asked to select ambigrams for different sections of the book: a case study section, which would feature process write-ups and sketches from the artists, and a showcase section, which would showcase several hundred unique entries. Along with the writing from several of the judges, this book would truly be one of a kind.

WHO THIS BOOK IS FOR

This book is intended for everyone. If you are an ambigrammist, you'll discover amazing new work and be able to connect with fellow artists (via their email or website). If you are a graphic designer, you'll love the typography and illustration. If you have never heard of ambigrams, you'll be amazed at the talent and creativity revealed in this art form. Regardless of which category you are part of, you'll find yourself flipping through the pages of this book for inspiration over and over again.

The writings and ambigrams that you'll see on the subsequent pages are a culmination of several years of writing, research, and design. This book is an international showcase of talent and a testament to the ambigram as an art form that pulls you in and does not let you go. You will get a glimpse inside the minds of different ambigrammists and learn how they think and work. Above all, after reading this book, you'll know what it takes to design an ambigram, and undoubtedly, will start sketching long before you get to the last page.

That being said, the time has come to turn the page and discover ambigrams for yourself. Enjoy the journey and the experience!

CHAPTER 1
A WORD FROM THE JUDGES

MEET NIKITA PROKHOROV

Nikita Prokhorov is a graphic designer, design professor, and the creative force behind *Ambigrams Revealed*. He has been freelancing as a designer for the last ten years and has worked as an advertising designer for *Scuba Diving* magazine. Currently, he lives and works in New York City. His identity work has been published in *HOW* magazine, Logolounge, and several other collections of identity and design books. For the past three years he has been developing content for and running Ambigram.com, the largest ambigram community in the world. In his time off from traditional graphic design, he pursues other creative passions, which are ambigrams, tessellations, and cooking. He is a minimalist at heart and has a soft spot for beautiful letterforms, hand-lettered typography, and propaganda-era posters.

THE ART OF THE AMBIGRAM

I have always been attracted to artists who forced me to look further past the surface of the canvas and deeper into my imagination. René Magritte's juxtaposition of unrelated objects and people left me speechless. The mythical landscapes of Salvador Dali's work let me wander within them for hours. Regardless of how frequently I saw the multiplanar and impossible realities of Maurits Cornelis Escher, I would walk away with a new discovery every time. Ambigrams embody illusion, mystery, and surprise, as Dali, Magritte, and Escher did with the worlds they created. Consequently, they caused you to look past your traditional knowledge and perception of typography and design, opening the door to something completely new.

What is it about an ambigram that makes it so mesmerizing? Is it the "eureka!" moment when you realize that by changing a word's orientation, you discover another word (*Figure 1.1*)? Is it how seamlessly it blends into the alphabet you are so used to reading, hiding among the letterforms and waiting for the right moment to surprise you? Or perhaps it is the process

Figure 1.1 You will most likely yell this when you discover your first ambigram!

of discovery and the ensuing desire to create one for yourself? Most likely, it is a combination of all of the above that pulls you in and does not let go.

LOOKING BEYOND THE ALPHABET

Ambigrams convey a certain aspect of illusion, but they are not magic. An ambigram is a puzzle with malleable pieces and multiple solutions. A traditional jigsaw puzzle has a set number of pieces that you assemble into a predetermined solution: Neither the puzzle pieces nor the final solution offer flexibility. But an ambigram has an undetermined number of typographic elements that you can shape and morph as you see fit for the best possible outcome. This is where the essence of the ambigram development process becomes clear. The exploration process guides how those typographic pieces will develop. Therefore, the perception of the final solution that you had at the start of the design process will change as well. It is nearly impossible to predict where the process will take you. As an ambigram designer, you are not just crafting new letters. You are establishing new relationships through existing letters. Each of those letters consists of a shape and meaning you learn from an early age. When you're crafting those new relationships, you have to take special care to preserve the original meaning. As we begin to delve deeper into the ambigram development process, let's first take a look at a few existing relationships within a traditional typeface.

Myriad Pro, a widely available and versatile typeface used in the design industry, has been set in 26 uppercase and lowercase letters (*Figure 1.2*). To demonstrate several rotational and reflective symmetries, it has also been divided into the following color-coded categories (*Figure 1.3*):

- **Red letters.** Red letters have perfect rotational symmetry. Regardless of whether you rotate them 180 or 360 degrees, they remain the same.

- **Yellow letters.** The yellow group of letters is a precursor to symbiotograms, a type of ambigram that when rotated 180 degrees, reveals a word that's different from the original. When rotated or mirrored, each letter reveals a different letter without any alteration.

abcdefghijklmnopq
rstuvwxyz

ABCDEFGHIJKLMNO
PQRSTUVWXYZ

Figure 1.2 Myriad Pro set in 26 uppercase and lowercase letters.

O S X Z
b d n M
a h C D
w P
f k E

Figure 1.3 Most letters within a traditional Latin alphabet have built-in symmetry, which is needed for a successful ambigram.

Figure 1.4 xpedx uses an ambigram for its corporate identity. It is easy to read, has a very strong presence in color or black/white, and is a perfect fit for the company. (xpedx and the xpedx logo are registered trademarks of International Paper.)

sins

siᴎs

siᴎs

chump

chump

chump

Figure 1.5 For each of these nearly natural ambigrams, only minor changes were needed. The top line in each group shows the word set in the original typeface. The middle line shows the changes made to half of the word with the original half of the word in gray. The bottom line shows the final solution. Notice how the aesthetic of the original typeface (Myriad Pro) was preserved.

• **Green letters.** When green letters are rotated, they closely resemble existing letters in their original orientation. However, they require slight modifications to be clearly perceived as such.

• **Blue letters.** Blue letters send mixed signals! When you turn the lowercase w 180 degrees, it becomes an uppercase M! When you turn the uppercase P 180 degrees, it becomes a lowercase d!

• **Orange letters.** Orange letters don't have conclusive symmetry and do not become other letters when rotated or reflected. However, they can be altered to represent other letterforms or can be used together with other characters to create recognizable elements.

Of course, not every letter of Myriad Pro was classified into the aforementioned categories. So grab a piece of paper, a pen or pencil, and start drawing and rotating the remaining letters to find out where they fit in.

Now that you know certain letters have naturally occurring symmetry, you may be wondering what happens if you arrange these letters into words? Well, these words are known as natural ambigrams: SOS, pod, and wow are just a few examples. There are also words that are almost natural ambigrams and require only minor tweaks. One of the best examples of a corporate identity that uses an ambigram is xpedx (*Figure 1.4*). Aside from minor alterations to the e, it's as close to a natural ambigram as possible. Aesthetically, it represents the company well, coming across as efficient, sturdy, and reliable. The transformation of a word that's nearly a natural ambigram isn't very difficult: You can quickly create an ambigram based on an existing typefeace while retaining all the properties of the original typeface (*Figure 1.5*).

CREATING AN AMIBIGRAM

The running joke among my colleagues and friends when they complain about their inability to read my ambigrams is that I suggest they do a handstand, and voilà!—instant legibility! If you are a designer new to this amazing art form, keep the following in mind: Not every word can become a good ambigram.

At times, no amount of sketching and Bezier curve wrangling will make the word legible and aesthetically sound. The success of your ambigram depends on many factors, but it begins with the word choice and letterform analysis. At the end of your design process, if it is difficult to read, it's not an ambigram; it's a typographic experiment. Not all experiments are successful, but although the design may be a failure as an ambigram, you still walk away with knowledge that you can incorporate into the next design. When you start drawing ambigrams, select simple words that require little typographic manipulation so you can learn the established relationships between the letters. In the initial stages you should be concerned with function first and aesthetics second. Forcing a visual style early on will make your effort a typographic experiment rather than a successful ambigram.

Take a look at the name "emilio" set in lowercase Helvetica Neue in *Figure 1.6a*. I selected Helvetica for this example due to its classic letterforms and proportions. Usually, I never base an ambigram on a typeface because that limits certain stylistic choices. The style of the ambigram manifests itself throughout the development process and should never be set in stone beforehand. When you base your design on an existing typeface, you trap yourself in a corner if the chosen word requires extensive letter manipulation, which doesn't always preserve the proportions and design of the typeface. In some cases, such as nearly natural ambigrams, the simple ambigram (shown in this example) can use certain elements of an existing typeface without compromising its structure and readability.

emilio

Figure 1.6a The name Emilio set in lowercase Helvetica.

Figure 1.6b Initial analysis identifies the most favorable letter-to-letter ratios.

INITIAL ANALYSIS OF EMILIO

Even at a passing glance, you see that the word emilio is an ambigram blessing in disguise. The word ends and begins with two round letterforms; therefore, the first obvious letter combination is the e/o. The remaining letters make a great matchup due to their strong verticals, so the only possible combination remaining is m/ili (*Figure 1.6b*). The dotted line in the center indicates a perfect central split, which shows

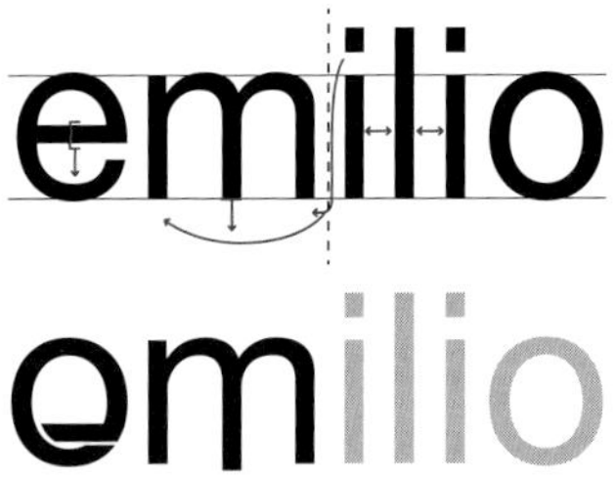

emilio

emilio

Figure 1.6c In-depth analysis shows changes needed to the existing typeface to turn it into an ambigram, while preserving the original typeface design and proportions as much as possible.

emilio

Figure 1.6d The finished ambigram.

emilio
emilio

Figure 1.6e Two variants of the emilio ambigram based on existing typefaces.

you have to alter one half of the word and then rotate it 180 degrees to complete the ambigram. You can see that it will take minimal changes to turn this word into an ambigram.

THE PROCESS

Even with the simplest ambigrams, you must respect existing letter proportions and relationships. While you're working on one side of the word, be careful not to distort the other! For the m/ili combination, notice that the m is the wider letter; a good approach would be to maintain the space between the ili so when it is rotated, it is as wide as the m. Adding the dots above the i and extending the center vertical stem of the m to make it look like the lowercase l completes the m/ili flip. The e/o transformation is just as simple. The crossbar of the e has to be lowered and disconnected on the left side to bring it closer to the appearance of the o (*Figure 1.6c*). Copying and rotating the first half finishes the ambigram (*Figure 1.6d*)! As you can see from this example, the combination of a well-designed typeface, a cooperative word, and some in-depth analysis laid the groundwork for an easy initial ambigram. The same formula can be applied to several more typefaces, which, although a bit more complex than Helvetica, yield virtually the same result—a legible and aesthetically sound ambigram. The letterform structure of the original word wasn't very complex so was morphed into an ambigram with relative ease.

For practice, try experimenting with other existing typefaces (*Figure 1.6e*) to see how the design and style of the typeface affects the legibility of the ambigram. Once your analytical and drawing skills develop further, you will understand that to create a truly unique ambigram, it's always a great idea to start on paper, allowing the developmental process of the ambigram to determine the final style (*Figure 1.6f*).

THERE IS NOTHING MORE PERSONAL AND INTIMATE FOR A LETTERING ARTIST THAN DRAWING A GOOD LETTER.

THINK OUTSIDE THE SOFTWARE

Now that you have created an ambigram or two, you've laid a cornerstone for a new passion that's likely to stay with you. But like any passion, it needs creative fuel, which is something you won't find within any software program. One of the biggest challenges new ambigrammists face is the speed with which they transition to the computer. Although drawing software offers a level of refinement for your final product, it will not replace the foundational elements that every designer needs. Let's review those essential elements next.

RESEARCH TOPOGRAPHY

At their core, ambigrams are typographic manipulation, and as such, are rooted in traditional typography. To learn the basics, it's best to take a typography and a calligraphy course at your local university. Study classic typefaces to understand their structure and design. Visit old bookstores and look at old typographic specimens as well as rare and out-of-print books. Carry your camera with you and take photographs of old hand-painted signs and graffiti on the sides of buildings. Use the computer to browse typography forums and lettering blogs, and of course, look at work by other ambigram designers. But don't just browse aimlessly: Observe and analyze words to figure out how they function.

SKETCH AND SKETCH, AND SKETCH SOME MORE

To an ambigram designer, sketching is as important as air. Sketch as much as you can every day! Keep a sketchbook with you at all times and imitate typography on signs, billboards, vintage packaging, and old ephemera. Sketch outside of your comfort zone. Draw what you aren't used to or comfortable with drawing; it will train your eye and hand. Initially, you will be tempted to digitize your work after only a few rough sketches, and you will struggle to re-create those sketches. The combination of your hands and eyes

Figure 1.6f If you want to create a truly unique ambigram, paper and pencil should be your starting point. A sketch of the ambigram is on top, and the vector version is on the bottom.

ambigram ambigram _{am}**bigr**_{am}

Figure 1.7 The word on the left is legible and readable due to balanced spacing, consistent size of the letters, and their positioning on the same baseline. The middle word is somewhat readable but not very legible due to the letter overlap. The word on the right is legible but difficult to read because of the difference in letter size and the fact they're not on the same baseline.

is a sophisticated drawing tool unlike any software program. It is a direct connection to your mind, unfiltered and unaffected by the digital medium. There is nothing more personal and intimate for a lettering artist than drawing a good letter. The more refined your final sketches are, the easier it will be to re-create them digitally.

Your understanding of letterform structure and drawing ability will improve as you continue to research and sketch. Throughout this process, you will realize that for a truly unique ambigram you should always start with paper and pencil, letting the development process guide you. As you continue to explore and analyze various ambigram solutions, you should focus on several elements:

• **Context.** From early childhood, you learn to identify letters and associate sounds with them. However, without combining them into words and learning how they work in context, those sounds and meanings may not make much sense. An ambigram functions in a similar manner. Although it is important to consider the meaning of an individual character or a pairing of letters, remember that they have to function well within the context of your chosen word.

• **Legibility vs. Readability.** Just as the yin and yang are complementary to each other, so are legibility and readability. They are interdependent and cannot function without each other. Legibility describes how you can perceive the different letterforms, and readability refers to how well-grouped letterforms can be recognized as words (*Figure 1.7*), sentences, and paragraphs. In any ambigram, the following factors can affect legibility and/or readability:

- Consistency and similarity between the lettering structure and style
- Proportions and proximity of the letterforms
- Negative space between the letters and words
- Color and texture
- Additional graphic elements that you may introduce as part of your design
- How overlapping parts of one letter can enhance or diminish your perception

All of these factors (except the last one, which is more relevant to the world of ambigrams) apply to traditional typography. A traditional typeface based on a 26-letter Latin alphabet is read in only one direction. An ambigram is viewed in different orientations and from different perspectives. Consequently, all the aforementioned factors take on a more vital role.

- **Letter ratios.** As you saw in the "emilio" example, an ambigram contains different letter ratios. The e/o flip is a 1-to-1 ratio. The m/ili flip is a 3-to-1 ratio: This ratio is less common than a 1-to-1 or a 2-to-1 ratio. These examples, as well those in *Figure 1.8*, showcase different letter ratios. Almost every word has the potential for different letter-to-letter ratios: Some of these may stand on their own but may not work within the context of the ambigram. Other ratios may work within the word, but take them out of context and they lose their meaning. Experimenting with different combinations on paper is the only way to account for all possibilities. You will not know whether a certain combination of letters will work until you try it!

- **Computers and software.** The computer and drawing software should be given their due. Although they are not an integral part of the initial development (with the exception of research), they play an important role in the closing stages of the design process and preparing your design for production and printing. In that regard, computers cannot be replaced: But they should not replace the brainstorming and development process.

Figure 1.8 Italia (top) is composed from 2-to-1 letter ratios, while Klimt (bottom) uses 3-to-2 letter ratios.

IN CLOSING

As you've seen and read, creating an ambigram is a complex blend of design and typography. On the following pages, you will read insightful writing from the other judges, as well as view beautiful examples of work from around the world. You will realize that each ambigram is unique and that the design process is very personal for each designer. Although there are certain standards that all ambigram designers should follow, at some point everyone deviates to the path of their individual process. Getting to that individual path requires a lot of thought, research, process, and determination. Once you get to that point, you will fall in love with this amazing art form, as all of us have.

MEET JOHN LANGDON

Award-winning logo designer and, along with Scott Kim, one of the originators of the ambigram art form, John Langdon is the creator and author of *Wordplay*, his book of and about his ambigrams. John created the iconic ambigrams in Dan Brown's best seller, *Angels & Demons*. His paintings of words have appeared in art gallery and museum exhibitions in the United States and Europe, and his ambigrams have been inked on bodies around the world. John's most recent wordy project is a complete rewrite of Lewis Carroll's *Alice in Wonderland*, featuring hundreds of subtle references to rock-and-roll history.

Although John's artwork has taken the form of corporate logos, ambigrams, paintings, and constructions, there are a few themes that unite those several forms of expression. The primary commonality is ambiguity. "I experience the world as being open to interpretation, and I see that each person's vantage point is valid and his or her reality is unique. In my work I try to share with the viewer the excitement that comes from exploring multiple viewpoints." Words and ideas are John's inspiration and subject matter. Symmetry is almost always present in John's work in one form or another.

John's genetic heritage bequeathed him almost equal portions of affinity for visual and verbal expression. As a result, the visual treatment of words comes naturally to him. Salvador Dali was his earliest significant inspiration. But the late 60s provided him with a number of powerful influences: the yin and yang symbol, M.C. Escher, psychedelic poster art and lettering, and Herb Lubalin's highly creative use of conventional typography. John teaches Advanced Typography in the Graphic Design program at Drexel University.

AMBIGRAMS: STARTING FROM SCRATCH

My career began with type. I graduated from college with a degree in English, no particular career direction, and an interest in advertising. It was how I thought artists made a living. With no portfolio or relevant education, I started at the bottom of the industry: in the camera department of Headliners, franchised in Philadelphia at Walter T. Armstrong Typography. But the beginnings of what I do began long before that. My grandfather was a poet and Romance language professor, my grandmother, a fine art painter. My dad taught penmanship. It seems that genetically I was predisposed toward the visual presentation of language.

Headliners was a photo-lettering business. As the name implied, all display type, all the time—24/7. But in the back there were guys melting down vats full of lead type for the linotype machines that droned like cicadas day and night. In 1970, computer-assisted photocomposition was barely even in existence. There was a typositor in one room, but typositor-set type was considered inferior to the headings that were assembled using letters individually cut out, and arranged by hand and tweezers on a piece of white cardboard covered with dried one-coat rubber cement (*Figure 1.1*).

Having never been conscious of type in my life, the idea of dozens of file cabinets filled with thousands of styles boggled my mind. But at an 8-hour-a-day pace, you learn fast. At first, with the exception of Bookman Swash, it all looked pretty much the same to me. And then Lubalin, Smith, and Carnase released its first bunch of display faces: Besides Avant Garde, there was Grizzly, Tom's Roman, Machine, and Grouch. The names reflected something a bit more lively than Standard Extrabold Condensed, Folio Extended, and

Figure 1.1 A sample of photolettering in process.

News Gothic Regular. I was already an *Avant-Garde* subscriber, so a connection was made between type and weird, countercultural attitudes and art.

Weird images had always appealed to me. The first art images that captured my imagination were Dali's surrealist mindscapes. And I was fascinated by M.C. Escher's work—with tiled, form-filling shapes, alternate frames of reference, and striking symmetries.

I graduated from the camera department in a few months and began working at a drawing board, cutting out letters for a setter, cleaning up the first-off prints, and preparing them for final shots. In between I discovered the industry publications *Graphis*, *Communication Arts*, and the latest promotion of lunatic psychedelic typefaces from *Lettergraphics* (which, at the time, I thought were great), which reminds me, I was a huge fan of psychedelic poster lettering. I imitated it on the envelopes of the letters I sent to my fiancée when she was still in college after I graduated.

As I began looking at art directors' club annuals, it was the logo sections that held my attention. Logos were highly concentrated devices, packing lots of information into an amazingly concise package. I had always enjoyed symbolism in literature, and here it was in gorgeously designed graphic form. By this time I had learned to use a T-square, triangle, rapidograph pen, and Pro white with a Windsor-Newton Series 7 number one brush—everything you need to be able to design logos!

The national headquarters of Headliners designed and promoted new typefaces several times a year. One typeface, Neo-Suisse Sans, caught my attention because several of the letters were designed to be exact inversions of other letters. The n and the u were identical, as they were in many sans serif faces, but so were the e and the a! Here was a typeface that reminded me of some of Escher's invertible images. By the time I had been at Headliners for a year, I was fascinated by

NEPTUNE YACHTS

Figure 1.2a This logo employs clever use of symmetry and reflection to create two different letters from one character. (Mark Dieterich)

Figure 1.2b Logo design for Elizabeth Ann Stallone.

Figure 1.3 If you saw these players right-side up before the game, you'd simply see that their numbers were 77 and 34. But in the heat of competition, a different message appears.

some of the creative opportunities type offered.

I began designing logos using the initials of many of my co-workers. George Hornbostel, a lettering artist in the role of a type salesman, encouraged and advised me. The late 60s and early 70s were a time of great corporate logo design. Most of the logos that attracted my attention cleverly united two letters into a single icon (*Figure 1.2a*). Others simply created one form that looked like both letters simultaneously. Some great ones used symmetry as an appealing aesthetic feature. I wanted to do stuff like that and found that it came to me somewhat naturally (with a lot of work). One personal logo from that era sticks in my memory: my first rotationally symmetrical design using the initials of one of my co-workers—Elizabeth Ann Stallone (*Figure 1.2b*; I was very good with the T-square, angle, and rapidograph pen but had yet to learn to draw freehand curves).

But my days at Armstrong were drawing to an end. My body was working at a type house, but my mind was busy becoming a logo designer. I had seen graphic design as my future and had to leave the type shop behind.

There are numerous small and seemingly innocuous experiences from my childhood that stuck in my head for some reason, and now, in retrospect, seem closely linked to my later development of ambigrams. A cartoon from a football game program (*Figure 1.3*; redrawn here from memory) is one of the earliest I can recall. The fact that 1961 could be read either way seems to have been more important to me than to most people. My childhood rock collection grew into a fascination with the symmetry systems of mineral crystals.

In college I discovered the mind-blowing images of M.C. Escher and the yin and yang symbol. They both spoke volumes to me about the idea of alternative points of view. And of course, in the late 60s and early 70s there were many cultural movements that questioned the status quo and traditional, conventional thinking.

My leisure time for the next twentyish years was spent filling hundreds of sheets of graphics paper and sketchbook pages with explorations of all kinds of optical illusions involving representational images, symbols, and letterforms. I deconstructed and reconstructed the yin and yang symbol in dozens of ways. But professionally, I was fixed on designing logos.

I learned a lot from the great logo designers of the early 70s, but two logos in particular caught my attention. Raymond Loewy's NEW MAN logo and Dick Hess's VISTA design for Volunteers in Service to America took full advantage of the ambiguity inherent in certain letters and typefaces but somehow did not propel me directly into ambigrams. I had been trying to force letters into tiled figure-ground relationships like Escher's birds and fish.

The totally natural forms of Loewy's six letters and the minimal alterations of forms in the VISTA logo must have allowed me to pass them over as incredibly happy coincidences—something to be hoped for and discovered rather than manipulated and wrestled into submission. But one night I wrote the word HEAVEN on my sketch pad. When I saw it later upside down, I realized that with a few little tweaks it could read the same both ways. In the next few moments, HELL and GOD had followed suit.

The next several weeks were an almost frantic exploration of my entire vocabulary, looking for more of these amazing opportunities. I tried the days of the week, months of the year, and the names of every friend and acquaintance I could think of. Most words resisted, but just enough were willing to cooperate to keep me obsessed (*Figure 1.4*).

A significant breakthrough came when I realized that when one letter refused to roll over and play, another letter or sometimes combining parts of letters, would do the trick. The CT/R glyph (*Figure 1.5*) was probably my first use of such a thing.

Soon my friend Bob Petrick had caught the

Figure 1.4 An early ambigram.

VICTORIA

Figure 1.5 One of the first uses of the 2-to-1 letter combination.

STARSHIP

Figure 1.6 An early example of bilateral, mirror image symmetry.

ambigram bug, and for a while we competed for intellectual property rights over certain reversal opportunities. Like Braque and Picasso, our friendly competition fueled our creativity. We had been cruising the streets of Philadelphia at lunchtime looking for small retail businesses that might be in need of a corporate identity makeover. But in time we raised our sights toward a burgeoning facet of the economy where the clients might be open-minded to some highly innovative designs: rock groups. For the most part they turned out to be harder to reach than most corporate entities and not necessarily any easier to work with. But Bob was able to sell one of his early ambigrams to a group called Angel. I had been trying for days or weeks to get the name STARSHIP to accede to my wish that it invert, and it teased me; every attempt came close, but nothing quite worked. Finally, it was just a question of listening to it rather than trying to force it. It became the first ambigram with bilateral, mirror-image symmetry (*Figure 1.6*).

I eventually sold the design to Jefferson Starship, but in the end it was almost not worth the effort. Rock musicians were commonly surrounded by layers of impenetrable bureaucratic management. It became clear that it was not really a very productive use of our time to design ambigrams on spec and then try to sell them. I began to focus more of my time on developing as a graphic designer and logo design specialist. But in the evening, those profuse and open-ended explorations continued, and every now and then a rotational gem would be the result. I had lost interest in making ambigrams of arbitrarily selected words and names. With little meaning and little commercial value, there seemed to be little reason to do so. But I maintained my enthusiasm for words whose meanings could be directly tied to the dualistic nature of the symmetrical graphic form (*Figure 1.7*).

Although it was hard to sell an ambigram, it was easy to give them away in the form of self-promotional mailers. And when one of those gems appeared, my wife and I would say, "That one should be in the book." The book was still more than ten years away. In fact, somebody else's book came out first. I picked up a copy of *OMNI* in November of 1979 and was stunned to find ambigrams in Scot Morris's "Games" column. Petrick and I had been sure that we were the only ones in the universe creating these things. A young computer science graduate student at Stanford University named Scott Kim had

Figure 1.7 The dualistic nature of the ambigram is potrayed by this Philosophy example.

designed a number of words that could be read the same both right-side up and upside down. He called them "inversions," which was also the name of Scott's soon-to-be-published book of invertible words. (The term ambigram, which I've been using anachronistically in this article, had not yet been coined. Bob and I had simply referred to them as "upside-down words." How boring!)

Feeling like I had been scooped, I turned my private creative efforts toward a number of paintings and constructions that manifested many of the ideas my yin and yang explorations had yielded. As part of that body of work, I commissioned the fabrication of two sizeable wall-hung turntables on which were silk-screened the PHILOSOPHY and the INFINITY ambigrams.

When I began teaching at Moore College of Art in the mid 80s, I was invited to show that work in the faculty gallery. A local publicist owed me a favor and got the local ABC TV station to do a brief spot about the work. The ambigrams were of particular interest. The parent network took notice and the spot was expanded for a short piece on *Good Morning America*. A small "new age" publisher in California saw the piece on TV and called to see if I would be interested in doing a book. (Ya gotta love it when it works that way!)

The answer was obviously a big Yes! But feeling like I didn't have enough ambigrams of "book" quality, I started working on new ones at a great rate, even as contract negotiations were under way. Those negotiations eventually broke down, but by that time the book had become real in my mind and prominent on my priority list. Things didn't fall into place all that well for a while. I did my share of knocking on publishers' doors and fielding rejection slips. But eventually, with a recommendation from Douglas

Figure 1.8 Wordplay was first published in 1992 with an expanded second edition to follow in 2005.

Hofstadter, I got to the right person at the right publishing house, and in 1992, *Wordplay* (Three Rivers Press) was published (*Figure 1.8*).

Wordplay sold respectably, but did not become a best seller. Bookstores never even figured out what section to place it in, and it did not, as I had fantasized, change my life in any significant way at all. The early 90s recession had taken hold while I had been writing the book, and the Macintosh had begun to revolutionize the graphic design world. Although I retained the 5 percent of my work that were corporate logo projects, the remainder—customized typography and hand lettering—disappeared overnight because the cutting-edge look of anything done on a Mac became the look that art directors and account execs wanted. I added to my teaching load and life went on, apparently with Wordplay and ambigrams as highlights in my rearview mirror.

But *Wordplay* caught the attention of a math professor named Dick Brown, and a few years later his son decided to write a novel. Dan wondered if I could do an ambigram of the title, *Angels & Demons* (Pocket Books, 2001) (*Figure 1.9*). Doing ambigrams on demand can be pretty iffy. I'm not exactly certain whether or not some words are just impossible to render into ambigrams. It seems to depend on incentive and time. In theory, I think that there are words that can't be done. But whenever I have felt that my reputation as an innovative lettering artist is on the line, or when it's just a stimulating challenge or exciting opportunity, if there's enough time to do an open-ended amount of exploration, I've been successful. The opportunity to have an ambigram on the front of

Figure 1.9 The book title for *Angels & Demons*.

Figure 1.10 Ambigrams commissioned for *Angels & Demons*.

a novel was exciting, and besides, the title reminded me of one of my favorite Escher engravings.

It took a long time, but Dan was thrilled with it, and he was able to convince the publisher that it had to be on the cover. That was pretty exciting, but I later found out how important it was that the title be an ambigram. Dan had in mind that significant turning points in the plot would occur around more ambigrams—ambigrams that had been created ages ago by mysterious artists in the employ of the Illuminati (*Figure 1.10*).

Sometimes I just get lucky. If someone said he wanted a specific group of words to be designed as ambigrams and that they had to all be done in a relatively uniform style, I'd say there was no way. Oh, and then if he said that when you've done them all individually, could you weave them into one four-word hyper-ambigram, well, surely I would say there is no way that could be done. And yet, somehow, that's how it worked out.

Happily, when *Angels & Demons* was first published in 2000, it sold better than *Wordplay*. I got paid and got a little more notice for that ambigram than for others I had done, and life went on. I felt that the time had come to really devote myself to painting, and turning the same ideas that had informed my ambigrams and my yin and yang constructions into paintings has been my top priority for the past several years. But ambigrams just keep on coming back for more. Dan's fourth novel, *The DaVinci Code* (Anchor, 2006), was so successful that it has reached back and coattailed *Angels & Demons* into the best-seller realm as well. And so, after only 30-some years, ambigrams have become pretty well known around the world.

THE ACTUAL NUTS AND BOLTS OF CREATING ROTATIONAL AMBIGRAMS

I begin an ambigram project by writing out the word freehand: For the example in *Figure 1.11*, I'm using a typeset version. Then I look at the word upside down. I have learned to write upside down just to save the trouble of having to invert my sketchbook every time. In this cap and lowercase setting, G and the E are both round and share the all-important center horizontal

Guthrie

Guthrie

Figure 1.11 Although this is a typeset version created on the computer, learning how to write upside down couldn't hurt!

ij u

Figure 1.12 Even before any adjustments are made, you can see that this letter combination has a lot of potential.

stroke. I'll have to alter the circular stroke and the horizontal, but it looks doable. As you'll see, a lot of the critical decision making revolves around two questions: How much can be taken away from a traditional letterform without losing its essence and its recognizability, and its corollary, how much can be added?

The G/E is an optimistic start, but the rest is much less encouraging. It doesn't look easy to make a u out of an upside-down i. But wait; looking at the r and i together, and imagining them actually moving closer together and then inverting them, they become very much like the letter u (*Figure 1.12*). Now just the t and h remain, and by extending the little curl at the bottom of the t, it can join the main stem of the h in a very natural way. By extending both legs of the h and crossing the second one, I've found the structural solution to the whole word.

Again, with the G/E glyph, what can I eliminate without losing the identity of the letter? With the critical and defining part of the G being the central horizontal stroke and the way it relates to the parts above and below it well represented, I find that the left side of the G is expendable, which is good because I need that part open to make the E. And because we read the tops of letters more than the bottoms, that little notch in the bottom of the u and the extended verticals of the h aren't really detrimental to readability at all. I've also added the principle that it's often necessary to combine two letters to make one facing the other direction.

The Guthrie ambigram (*Figure 1.13*) makes for a good demonstration because of the simplicity of the letter styles. But it should be noted that I never begin by using an existing typeface (font). I always let the letters evolve in pencil-sketch form. It's worth noting that typefaces are designed according to principles— rules, virtually—developed and established over many centuries of calligraphic and typographic traditions. Except for those few words like NOON, ambigrams require that those rules be set aside, at least temporarily. As a rule, words only read from one vantage point. As a rule, a letterform only needs to represent one sound. As we attempt to create words in ways the alphabet never had in mind, we have to subvert those conventions, and we have to be open-minded

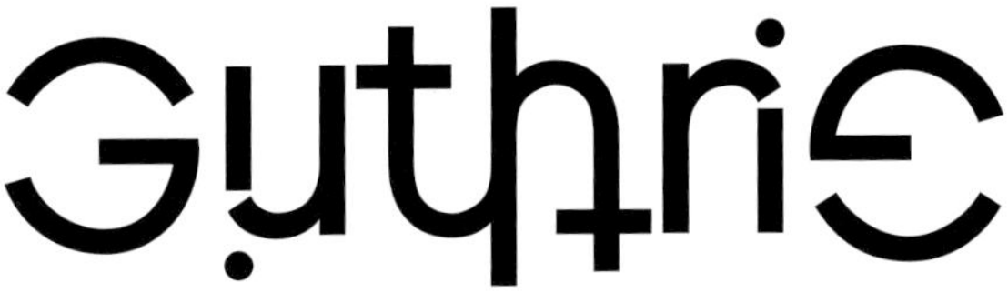

Guthrie

Figure 1.13 The finished ambigram.

to doing things we've always considered "wrong." Capital letters may need to be mixed with lowercase letters, for example, as you see in the form of the E in Guthrie.

But many ambigrams require more complex styles than Guthrie. The VICTORIA design (shown earlier) shows why some ambigrams call for the use of thick and thin strokes, and also, on occasion, decorative flourishes. (VICTORIA is the one ambigram for which I actually did use an existing font! It was an early ambigram, before I had much experience or confidence in drawing original letters.) The R in the font—University Roman—has a very unusual proportion with its rounded bowl much larger than normal and the diagonal leg greatly suppressed. That relationship between the parts of the R was very helpful in creating a C that was almost as large as the rest of the letters, and the leg of the R atop the letter C simply became a decorative flourish. In fact, it's not completely decorative, because I gave it the function of dotting the I. Because I introduced a "decorative" bit in one place, using more made that one seem more natural, more integrated. The VICTORIA ambigram shows that A's don't even need horizontal cross-strokes, but a second natural use here would be crossing the A with a flourish. The scrollwork inside the O was purely decorative but did create a faint reference to the yin and yang symbol—one of a few major influences that eventually led me to invent/discover ambigrams.

THE YIN AND YANG SYMBOL—ONE OF THE MAJOR INFLUENCES THAT EVENTUALLY LED ME TO INVENT/DISCOVER AMBIGRAMS

MEET SCOTT KIM

Scott Kim is an independent game designer who designs original visual thinking puzzles for the Web, computer games, magazines, and toys. Major projects include puzzles for the websites Adobe.com and Juniornet.com, the computer games Obsidian and Escher Interactive, the magazines *Discover* and *Games*, and the physical toy Railroad Rush Hour®.

His interest in puzzles sprang from an early interest in mathematics, education, and art. His first puzzles appeared in *Scientific American* in Martin Gardner's Mathematical Games column. Other pursuits include creating "inversions" (words that read in more than one way) and creating educational dance performances about mathematics.

He was born in 1955, raised in Los Angeles, and attended Stanford University, where he received a B.A. in music and a self-designed Ph.D. in Computers and Graphic Design. He currently lives in El Granada, California, near San Francisco, with his wife Amy (online community strategist and author of Community Building on the Web) and his son Gabriel. You can read more about his work on his website at www.scottkim.com.

BEYOND AMBIGRAMS

In 1975, I was taking my first graphic design class at Stanford University. I was familiar with palindromes, which are reversible words and sentences like RACECAR and WAS IT A CAR OR A CAT I SAW? And I knew of a few isolated examples of words that read the same upside down and right-side up, like the words NOON and pod or the sentence NOW NO SWIMS ON MON. But ambigrams as an expansive art form had not yet been born.

One of the class assignments asked me to do the following:

Produce a flat design in two or more colors that has no background: that is, one in which the spaces between forms are as positive as the forms themselves (as in a checkerboard). The objective is to make all of the parts of your composition interrelate—use all of the space and make it all work.

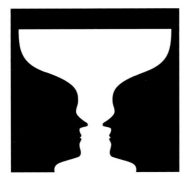

Figure 1.1 One of the most popular representations of the figure/ground principle.

Figure 1.2 The negative space within the capital R reveals a lowercase i.

Figure 1.3 The Figure/Figure ambigram.

For instance, in the widely reproduced example in *Figure 1.1* the positive white foreground forms a vase, and the negative black background forms profiles of two people looking at each other. The positive and negative forms are also called the figure and ground, respectively. Nothing in the class assignment suggested that I work with words, but for some reason I got it in my head to write the word FIGURE so the space around and between the letters would spell the word GROUND. My first attempt failed miserably, although I did notice that the I in FIGURE fit nicely inside the R in GROUND (*Figure 1.2*).

So I changed the problem. Rather than fit FIGURE and GROUND together, I tried fitting FIGURE together with an upside-down copy of itself, noting that crossbars of F fit nicely with the crossbars of an inverted E. *Figure 1.3* shows my second attempt.

Right-side up it reads FIGURE in black; upside down it reads FIGURE in white. Not bad; but I didn't like the weird bump on the bottom of the I, which helps define the R. So I changed the problem again. Rather than fit FIGURE with itself upside down, I tried fitting FIGURE with itself right-side up, shifted over three letters (*Figure 1.4*).

Notice that the I fits inside the R, just as I had noticed earlier, and that you can read the word FIGURE down as well as across. This solution pleased

Figure 1.4 A Figure/Figure tessellation.

me (and my teacher) enormously and made me wonder what other treasures lay waiting to be discovered in the land between mathematics and language.

My struggle to create the FIGURE/FIGURE figure (as Douglas Hofstadter called it) taught me several important lessons. First, work hard to make the ambigram legible. It is easy to fool yourself into thinking that a design is legible just because you can read it. But you already know what it says, so you are biased. Second, if one approach fails, then change the problem. I changed the FIGURE problem twice before I found a good solution. Third, let your desire to express the meaning of a word (or name) dictate the form of the solution. My search for a way to express the idea figure and ground led me to explore graphic construction that I never would have explored otherwise.

GETTING BETTER

After creating my first ambigram, I tried making ambigrams out of my friends' names. Most of my ambigrams were rotationally symmetric; a few were mirror symmetric. I showed my creations (*Figure 1.5*) to my friend Douglas Hofstadter, who in turn showed me ambigrams he had created many years earlier, which were inspired by his friend.

But after several years I became dissatisfied. My lettering was merely decent and didn't measure up to the professional lettering I so admired. So I took calligraphy classes, studied typography and type design, and joined the budding digital typography program at Stanford, which was led by computer science professor Donald Knuth. It was then that I learned to see like a lettering artist.

I poured my newfound knowledge into my book *Inversions* (Key Curriculum Press, 1996), which was published in 1981 (*Figure 1.6*). Although *Inversions* was the first published book of ambigrams, many other artists had already hit upon the same idea independently, most notably, John Langdon.

Figure 1.5 Some examples of my early ambigram work.

AMBIGRAMS REVEALED 25 A WORD FROM THE JUDGES • SCOTT KIM

CRAFTING A GOOD AMBIGRAM—ONE THAT READS WELL, AND RESONATES WITH BEAUTY—TAKES MUCH MORE WORK.

Figure 1.6 The title lettering for *Inversions*, published in 1981. Turn the word upside down and see what you can read!

In the last 30 years ambigrams have grown into a worldwide phenomenon. Articles about ambigrams first appeared in *OMNI* (1979) and *Scientific American* (1981) magazines. Then John Langdon's superb work appeared in Dan Brown's best-selling novel *Angels & Demons*, which was later made into a movie. Finally, the ambigram community got its own meeting place on the Web at ambigram.com, which was started by Mark Hunter and its curator and author of this book, Nikita Prokhorov. As you flip through the pages of this book, you will see excellent ambigrams from all corners of the globe.

CRITERIA FOR SUCCESS

Anyone who can read and write can write a word so it reads in more than one direction. For instance, try this introductory exercise: write USA so it reads both right-side up and upside down. All it takes is paper, pencil, persistence, and bit of luck. But crafting a good ambigram—one that reads well and resonates with beauty—takes much more work. I find that it takes me one or two days to turn a good idea into a finished ambigram—sometimes more. Here are the four qualities I look for in a good ambigram, as well as tips for achieving that level of quality:

1. LEGIBILITY

A good ambigram must read easily and clearly. Don't make the reader work hard to decipher what your ambigram says. Tips for maximizing legibility include:

• **Strive to find letter shapes that are clear and unambiguous.** If a particular letter shape just isn't working, consider using an alternate form of the letter; for instance, you can use a triangular capital A, a two-story lowercase a, or a one-story cursive a.

- **Use a consistent lettering style.** Strive for consistent case (all uppercase, all lowercase, or initial capital); mixed-case lettering is harder to read. Maintain consistent letter spacing and letter heights; jumbled lettering is harder to read.

- **Know what you can get away with.** The first letter of a word is the most important to get right. You can get away with later letters being less clear, because once viewers read the first few letters of a word, they will anticipate what comes next.

You can also get away with the bottom halves of letters being oddly formed, especially in lowercase, because the top halves of lowercase letters are where most of the information is. For instance, almost anything with a dot over it looks like an i, and almost anything with a crossbar looks like a t.

- **Study conventional fonts to understand how letters are normally formed.** For example, in an uppercase A, the right diagonal stroke is normally thicker (or the same thickness) as the left diagonal stroke; anything else looks strange.

- **Remember that you already know what your ambigram says, so you are not the best judge of its legibility.** Show your ambigram to other people without telling them what it says, and find out if they can read it.

2. APPEARANCE

A good ambigram should also look good. Lettering that obeys the conventions of good lettering will usually look good, but there are additional graphic tricks that can enhance the visual appeal of your design. Tips for improving appearance include:

- **Get the structure right first.** First, draw the bones of your lettering with a thin single-width line. Get the curves, shapes, and visual rhythm right before thickening the strokes and adding flourishes.

ONLY AFTER YOUR DESIGN WORKS IN BLACK AND WHITE SHOULD YOU CONSIDER ADDING COLOR, OUTLINES, SHADING, AND OTHER GRAPHIC EMBELLISHMENTS.

Figure 1.7 First attempt at an Annie ambigram.

Figure 1.8 A second (and better) solution for the Annie ambigram.

Figure 1.9 An example of a chain ambigram.

• **Trust your hand.** I typically draw an ambigram a dozen times quickly in pencil to find the best curves and letter shapes. Sometimes I work out designs directly on the computer, but working by hand is usually the best way to create forms that work organically together.

When you're judging the appearance of your ambigram, suppress the urge to read the word and focus instead on purely visual qualities, such as line weight, positive and negative shapes, and visual rhythm.

Only after your design works in black and white should you consider adding color, outlines, shading, and other graphic embellishments. Such additions can enhance the appearance of an ambigram, but they can't fix basic structural problems.

• **Be sure your graphic enhancements don't harm legibility.** On the other hand, graffiti and tattoos often deliberately flirt with illegibility as part of their charm.

3. PROBLEM SOLVING

A good ambigram should contain good solutions to the challenges inherent in the design. For instance, *Figure 1.7* shows a bad ambigram of the name ANNIE. The A/E letterform is awkward, leaving an unjustified extra stroke at the left of the E. The N/I letterform uses an I that has a lot of extra baggage and is therefore hard to read. Additionally, the letter spacing is terrible due to a vast canyon between the last two letters.

We can clean up the unsightly garbage between the I and the E by regrouping the strokes so the extra stroke on the E is justified as being the I (*Figure 1.8*). Now every stroke is justified, and the letter spacing is even—a better solution.

4. EXPRESSING MEANING

Sometimes it is possible to write a word so it expresses its meaning through its form. For example, the ambigram in *Figure 1.9* of the word INFINITY takes the form of an endless circle. When this can be done in a natural way that is integral to the lettering, the form and content of the ambigram bond to form a greater whole—the same way the lyrics and the melody of a good song bond to express something greater than either individually.

Although this extra of level of meaning is wonderful, it is not always attainable, or advisable. For instance, you can add illustrations of piano keys to an ambigram of the word "piano" to enhance its entertainment value, but it doesn't improve the quality of the ambigram. Some artists like to add this sort of embellishment; I tend to shy away from it. Instead, I prefer to try finding a form that adds to the meaning of the word without overt illustration. For instance, the HIYASHI ambigram shown on page 31 suggests a spider web and the eight legs of a spider without any extraneous elements.

BEYOND ROTATION AND REFLECTION

Most of the ambigrams in this book have either rotational symmetry—can be read right-side up and upside down—or reflective symmetry—can be read normally and as a mirror image. A few have other symmetries. The same breakdown of symmetries applies to my work: Most of my ambigrams have rotational symmetry, some have mirror symmetry, and a few have other symmetries.

Rotation ambigrams are the most common type of ambigrams for good reason. When a word is turned upside down, the top halves of the letters turn into the bottom halves. And because our eyes pay attention primarily to the top halves of letters when we read, that means that you can essentially chop off the top half of a word, turn it upside down, and glue it to itself to make an ambigram. Of course, there is more to making an ambigram than just copying and pasting, but just doing that works surprisingly well, as shown by the copy and paste job of the word "ambigram" in *Figure 1.10*.

Reflection ambigrams are pleasing because our visual system is wired to notice bilateral symmetry. Reflection ambigrams also have the magical property that allows them to be read as a mirror image. However, reflection ambigrams tend to be harder to create than rotation ambigrams, because the tops of letters stay tops of letters when reflected. Also, the

ambigram

ambigram

ambigram (reflected/rotated)

Figure 1.10 A simple copy-and-paste approach for creating an ambigram from the word "ambigram," albeit crude, works surprisingly well in this instance.

information information information

Figure 1.11 An example of a chain ambigram.

OHIO

Figure 1.12 An ambigram example that combines reflective and rotational properties.

LIGHT IS A

wave!

Figure 1.13 An oscillation ambigram. (Douglas Hofstadter)

conventional diagonal stress of letters like capital A and V gets reversed when the letter is reflected, as shown by the reflection ambigram on the palindromic name "AVIVA." (Thus, when I create reflection ambigrams, I avoid giving letters diagonal stress.)

But why stop there? Here is a quick tour of some of the other ambigrammatical hoops that words can jump through:

• **Chain ambigrams.** Instead of the middle of the ambigram being in the middle of the word, the center of rotation is displaced to one side, causing the word to repeat. A chain ambigram is fundamentally easier to create than a conventional ambigram, because being able to shift the center gives the creator many more choices when deciding which letters to turn into which other letters. *Figure 1.11* shows a chain ambigram of the word "information." The chain has to keep going because INFORMATION by itself inverts to FORMATIONIN.

• **Reflection + Rotation.** If we also allow words to be spelled vertically with letters stacked from top to bottom, there are about a dozen different ways that a word can be turned or reflected to read in a different direction—a taxonomy that Douglas Hofstadter humorously dubbed the "gramma sutra." For instance, the state name OHIO turns into itself if it is rotated 90 degrees counterclockwise, reflected about a horizontal mirror, or rotated 90 degrees counterclockwise and reflected about a vertical mirror (*Figure 1.12*).

• **Oscillation.** In this special sort of symbiotogram, a word turns into another word without being turned or reflected. It just sits there, oscillating between two interpretations without moving at all. *Figure 1.13* shows a profoundly expressive ambigram by Douglas Hofstadter that expresses the dual nature of light as revealed by physics.

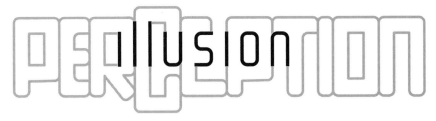

Figure 1.14 A containment ambigram.

Figure 1.15 A word cross created for Cheryl Hiyashi, who studies the chemistry of spider silk.

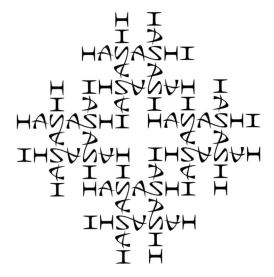

• **Containment.** Using containment, one word is part of another. It is similar to an oscillation, but some parts of the outer word play no role in the inner word; thus, this type of ambigram is easier to create (*Figure 1.14*).

• **Word Crosses.** In this design, words cross each other at 90 degree angles with letters at the intersections that function in more than one direction. Like containment ambigrams, word crosses are easier to create than conventional ambigrams, because some of the letters are free (not constrained to look like any other letter). I created the word cross in *Figure 11.5* for scientist Cheryl Hiyashi, who studies the chemistry of spider silk. The first, third, fifth, and seventh letters cross other letters; the letters in even-numbered positions are not constrained by crossings (although in this design I did constrain them to duplicate the shapes of other similar letters).

Figure 1.16 A bilingual symbiotogram. (David Moser)

Figure 1.17 The Chinese word for China in its original form.

- **Symbiotograms.** Instead of turning a word into itself, symbiotograms turn a word into another word. Symbiotograms are not fundamentally different from ambigrams that read the same both ways: A symmetrical ambigram is after all a symbiotogram that turns the first half of the word into the last half of the word. But symbiotograms often have a more powerful effect than symmetrical ambigrams, because one word appears to magically transform into another. For instance, the classic symbiotogram on page 124 by graphic designer C. E. Krausie transforms LIFE into DEATH.

- **Bilingual.** Another type of symbiotogram pairs words in different languages. Bilingual ambigrams are especially exciting when the two languages use different symbols, as in the English/Chinese symbiotogram in *Figure 1.16* by David Moser (he calls them "sinosigns"). To the right of the sinosign is the Chinese word for China in its original form (*Figure 1.17*; using the older unsimplified form of the character for "country"). Both the English and the Chinese read right-side up.

- **Other symbol systems.** You can even stray beyond the bounds of languages and work with numbers or other symbols. *Figure 1.18* shows a design I created on the name Schönberg, the composer who invented 12-tone composition in the early twentieth century (a system in which the notes of the scale are assigned numbers 1 through 12). Other than the 11 for the umlaut, all numbers appear at the same scale.

Figure 1.18 A symbol system based on a 12-tone composition.

- **Figure/Ground.** In a figure/ground design, letters fit together so the space around and between one word spells another word, as in the FIGURE/FIGURE figure shown earlier. Closely related to the incredible tessellating animals of artist M. C. Escher, *Figure 1.19* shows a spectacular typographic tessellation called Escher Pavage (Escher tiling) by French artist Alain Nicolas on the name Escher, which reads in four different directions.

- **Dissection.** With dissection, letters fit together like pieces of a jigsaw puzzle to make a shape. Dissection is a looser form of figure/ground in which the letters of a word can be moved or turned around before being assembled. *Figure 1.20* shows a dissection I created for the puzzle sculptor Miguel Berrocal. The letters have hefty geometric shapes similar to the pieces that make up his sculptures.

Figure 1.19 A figure/ground typographic tessellation. (Alain Nicolas)

Figure 1.20 A dissection ambigram.

Figure 1.21 A slide ambigram.

Figure 1.22 As this example shows, multiple solutions for the same word are possible.

• *Slide.* In a slide design, a word is composed of two copies of exactly the same design, one superimposed on the other with one copy slid to the right (*Figure 1.21*), such as the slide ambigram I created for digital artist John Maeda. This type of ambigram (if you can call it that) cannot be read in more than one way, unlike other ambigrams, but does follow an exact rule that constrains every part of every letter to copy a part of another letter. Slide ambigrams are similar to musical canons, like Frere Jacques, except that instead of one copy of the melody being displaced in time to form two-part harmony, one copy of the visual design is displaced in space to form a legible word. This sort of design works better as an animation or interactive piece than as a static image.

Besides changing the symmetry of an ambigram, you can also change the material. I've seen beautiful ambigrams constructed by quilting or carving stone, or constructed out of neon tubes, as on page 126.

In addition, you can increase the challenge by giving yourself less latitude in the choice of words. Douglas Hofstadter once created a series of ambigrams on the names of all the states in the USA. Not only did he create 50 ambigrams, but he did so without giving himself the freedom to skip any of the names.

You can also challenge yourself to find multiple solutions to the same word or phrase. *Figure 1.22* shows two ambigrams on Martin Gardner's Celebration of Mind, an annual event honoring the famed science/math/magic author. Each year I challenge myself to create a logo that reads as the name of the event one way and a different alliterative phrase, describing Gardner's work, upside down. It's an outrageous challenge, but that's how I like it. And as any ambigram maker can attest, finding a solution to such a difficult challenge is as magical for the person making it as it is for the person reading it.

MEET MAGGIE MACNAB

Maggie Macnab has been a strategically creative visual design communicator for over three decades and has owned Macnab Design since 1981. Her work has been recognized by leading design industry magazines and books, and has received both national and international honors. She teaches design theory at Santa Fe University of Art and Design, the Institute of American Indian Arts, the University of New Mexico, and the Santa Fe Community College, and is past president of the Communication Artists of New Mexico. Maggie also speaks at conferences, guest lectures at schools in the United States and abroad, and gives workshops on integrating symbolism into design. Her first design theory book, *Decoding Design: Understanding and Using Symbols in Visual Communication* (F+W, 2008), was released worldwide to critical acclaim and has received two awards. Her second, *Design by Nature: Using Universal Forms and Principles in Design* (Peachpit Press, 2011), has been translated into Spanish, Korean, Chinese, and Japanese. Maggie is committed to beautiful and functional visual communications and to creative global problem solving that recognizes nature as the primary design mentor. *Design by Nature* is a current finalist for Best Nonfiction and Reference from the New Mexico/Arizona Book Awards.

THE ORGANIC AMBIGRAM

The ambigram is one of the few modern letterforms that engages your intellect and intuition simultaneously. It reads as a word while also communicating a deeply familiar pattern. This is something beyond the ambigram's obvious clever construction. I've thought quite a bit about why I love this word–image hybrid, and in writing this I set out to uncover just what it is about the ambigram's design and structure that make it so charismatic.

My primary design background is as a symbolic logo designer, so I began with what I know: symbols. I look to nature to create my work as a matter of practicality as well as aesthetics because symbols are derived of nature and are the first language of all humans. Symbols engage us deeply as expressions of the organic principles and forms that life embodies. Nature is common to everyone, and when it is used symbolically in visual language, the chance of creating a relationship with the audience is significantly elevated because it mirrors the relationships within and around us. Nature even embeds symbols directly into our DNA that mirror universal processes (*Figure 1.1*). The twisting double helix is a perfect example of combining opposites into the genetic dance of balance, resulting in you and me. Unlike spoken or written language, natural symbols don't have to be learned because we know them at our core. They are us.

Art or design that incorporates natural symbolism resonates intuitively well before the intellect "makes sense" of it. Written language is processed intellectually first, before it is understood as images or emotions. Without doubt, much of the ambigram's personal appeal for me has to do with my visual-leaning preference for information that you can share. But it is something more universal than that. Ambigrams combine a word with the symbolic representation of a much larger principle. When you see reflection, oscillation, rotation, continuity, and other universal principles integrated as an intrinsic part of

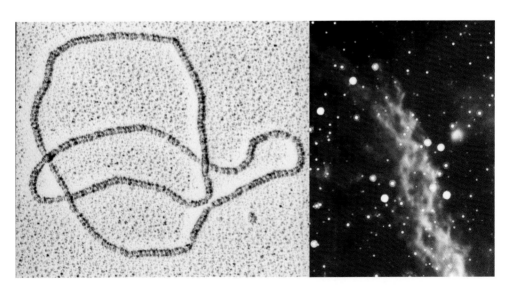

Figure 1.1 Micro to macro, a handful of patterns construct everything in the universe. The weaving pattern of the helix combines two opposites in cooperation, the basis of organic life. (DNA micrograph: Andrzej Stasiak. Double helix nebula at the center of the Milky Way galaxy: NASA, 2006)

Figure 1.2a The Paris ambigram has reflected (or mirror) symmetry. (Nikita Prokhorov)

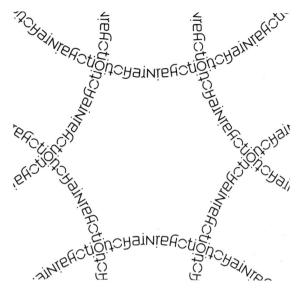

Figure 1.2b "Chain Reaction" displays weaving, continuity, and rotational symmetry. (John Langdon)

the design, it engages you at a deep level (*Figures 1.2a* and *1.2b*). Any piece of art or design that embeds a universal principle connects itself to something more, something real, and something we just know.

An ambigram takes on the same sort of life that a symbol does by connecting to nature, but how does it become its own entity, and such a visually lively one at that? To uncover that, you need to look at both parts of the ambigram: the word and the universal principle expressed. Although the written word is the most apparent component of the ambigram, you intuitively process visual information before you intellectually understand it, so let's start with image and intuition first.

SYMBOL-SPEAK

Humans have survived and proliferated by reading the universal principles and forms of nature as a common symbolic language, no matter when or where they lived. The principles that constitute a successful ambigram resonate to your depths because you are made up of the very same fundamental formulas. Your

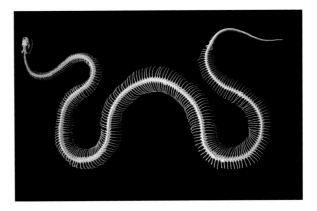

Figure 1.3 As the dominant symmetry of all higher life-forms, bilateral symmetry is a compelling and intuitively recognizable principle. (Snake skeleton: Draskovic/iStockphoto.com)

Figure 1.4 This six-meter long rock resembling a python, discovered in Africa in 2006, is embellished with more than 300 man-made "scales" and is approximately 70,000 years old. Humans have been using their brains symbolically since "time out of mind." (Photo by Sheila Coulson, Institute of Archaeology, Conservation, and History, University of Oslo, Norway)

intuition knows that a circle is the shape of wholeness or completion (planets, eggs, cells, molecules, seasonal cycles); that waves oscillate to balance extremes (atoms and galaxies do this, too); that the branching pattern (as tree branches, veins, lightning, or the network of nerves that drive impulses throughout your body) moves life's energy from one place to another; and that mirrored halves contain bilateral symmetry—the basic structural form of almost all higher animals (*Figure 1.3*), including the human body. When a universal principle becomes a primary ingredient of a piece of communication, be it literal or visual, something tells you to take note. The ambigram resembles independent, self-animated "life" by presenting the very same qualities.

Communication in the modern world has ramped up to a scale and speed never before possible, and the human species is now networked in the extreme. The Web connects the body of the world just as impulses connect throughout your body, but with one important difference: Common ground must be established in human communication because of so many cultural and lingual crossovers, unlike the immediate language of nature. Symbols help to do this by bringing an underlying fluency to people of different cultures and languages. They predate written language by at least tens of thousands of years and are far older than civilization itself. But because three-dimensional space is continually morphing, time erases nearly all traces. From what has been found to date (there is evidence of complex symbolic behavior going back as far as 200,000–500,000 years!), we know that our predecessors recognized the value of the information contained in natural patterns and forms all around us (*Figure 1.4*).

All cultures use the same shapes and patterns in their art because we all experience them in the same way. Everything we've ever invented has come from understanding a universal underlying process and then replicating it as a human system. City grids mimic the stacking and packing patterns of nature in a linear format; apartment buildings and shopping carts contain the same pattern of stored energy in three dimensions; and road systems that carry petro-fueled vehicles mimic veins that carry the energy that fuels our bodies (*Figure 1.5*). Patterns, shapes, and processes of the natural world cue our inspiration and understanding by revealing the eternal baseline of existence. You simply can't stop noticing nature's processes in your peripheral vision. As constants of organic structure, this presents an interesting paradox: The workings of nature are typically ignored by our sped-up intellect as commonplace but are recognized instantly by the senses as essential and eternal.

Figure 1.5 Nature's process dictates effective human design. Packing and stacking is another natural pattern that efficiently stores energy that isn't needed in the moment but is readily accessible. (John Langdon)

THE AMBIGRAM COMMUNICATES MORE THAN THE SUM OF ITS CHARACTERS BECAUSE IT IS ENHANCED WITH PRINCIPLES THAT COMMUNICATE BEYOND THE WORD ITSELF.

Language barriers preclude this ability to communicate universally and immediately. Visuals are immediate because they connect as a whole gestalt, and they communicate in universally and personally relevant ways. The ambigram communicates more than the sum of its characters because it is enhanced with principles that communicate beyond the word itself.

THE MANIPULATED AND THE MANIPULATOR

Words, as opposed to symbols, tend toward specifics (different words can describe multiple aspects of one thing) and can dissect meaning into smaller and smaller details. Words are particularly good at giving directions, stating rules, or declaring a law. Being created by humans, they are also malleable by humans. The way they are written can change lives, as is so often demonstrated in systemic religion, law, and politics. Written language is an essential human activity that not only provides information with efficient and (sometimes) consistent delivery, but it allows generations to communicate their stories over time.

The ambigram is a perfect example of inclusiveness, and the root of this word tells you so right up front. The word ambigram is derived from two Latin words joined as one, as are many modern words. The root *ambi-* means "both," and it is a popular prefix in a world of dualities, such as day/night, youth/age, left/right, birth/death, good/evil—words that provide the bounding markers of every human experience. Its suffix *-gram* is another Latin word meaning tracing, mark, drawing, writing, or record—a common addition to our vocabulary ever since humans started taking notes. All sorts of everyday words include the prefix *ambi* as an idea of all or inclusiveness. Ambient is combined with the Latin *-ier*, which means to go ("both" in this case includes everything in between extremes and surrounds you within your environment in a particular moment in time) and describes an ambiance that enhances a relaxed mood. Another word used in this context is ambition, or the act of moving around and through the multitudes. Ambition is originally derived from a Latin word for "canvassing for votes," and covering every base to reap the best return. The legal term ambit is derived from the Latin *ambitus*, meaning scope, limits, boundary, or circumference: The "ambit of a statute," or "within the ambit of the law" falls within legally defined bounds. Ambidextrous refers to both hands having equal dexterity. The Latin *dexter* means right, so two rights for those who are adept with using both hands—the lefties might have a say about that! To be ambivalent is to literally have either or both of two contrary or parallel values, qualities, or meanings (the Latin verb *-valeo* means "to have value"). By its very nature, ambi is inclusive of opposites and implies wholeness.

A LIVING LOOP

The ambigram's sublime evolution exists within the form of the actual word. The word must have visual relationships to be interesting and relevant, not only in the way the characters create a meaningful word, but also in the symmetrical relationships that let you know you are experiencing something beyond just a simple word. Ambigrams have the rather fantastic ability to be read upside down or backwards—and even sometimes in a spin (*Figure 1.6*)!

Figure 1.6 Called a "chain" ambigram, this design presents an infinite loop that mimics the underlying cyclical motion of life and death. (Scott Kim)

IN ANY BEAUTIFUL AND FUNCTIONING DESIGN— MAN-MADE OR NATURAL—BALANCE REIGNS SUPREME.

By visually expressing some of the most basic principles that make up the entirety of living, organic nature, ambigrams mimic life. There is one fundamental necessity that underscores all the various symmetries and structures an ambigram can take on, and that is *balance*. In any beautiful and functioning design—man-made or natural—balance reigns supreme. Modern culture could learn from this: The opposite sides of your brain are not meant to contradict and entangle without resolution. Being creative is not of more or less value than being strategic. They are meant to work together. The same goes for opposite sides of the world's hemispheres. When opposites combine in cooperation, they create something new, something useful, and something beautiful that is far stronger and more resilient than favoring one over another.

Regardless of the rather incredible technological advances the current era of humanity has made, we still lag behind our ancestors in understanding an important lesson displayed by the simple ambigram. We are nature and cannot put ourselves above our source, nor can we distance ourselves from it for very long. When you see a piece of design that just simply makes you feel good, what you're really seeing is an expression of nature flowing in place. It feels right because the common denominators that underscore all life are the truest part of the human experience. It's the most compelling reason there is. Ambigrams are closed living loops; they are little word ecosystems that stand independently on their own, just as each of us are designed to do.

MEET CHERYL SAVALA

Proud to stand alongside gifted artists, authors, and filmmakers who create timeless and heartfelt stories, Cheryl leads the creative crew at Menagerie Creative, an entertainment design and marketing agency. For over 20 years Cheryl has orchestrated, designed, and occasionally illustrated the creative and marketing campaigns for several of our culture's most beloved films, including The *Star Wars Saga*, *Titanic*, *The Sound of Music*, *Planet of the Apes*, and *The Princess Bride*. Her passion for mentoring creative professionals is shared through her workshops and collegiate courses in lettering, personal branding, and the emotional language of entertainment design.

THE POETRY AND SYMPHONY OF AMBIGRAMS

As long as I can remember, I've had an infatuation with the illustrative word. Illuminated manuscripts, vintage movie posters, and 80s record jackets all inspired my experimentation with lettering design. Then one excursion to a local book store uncovered John Langdon's *Wordplay*, and the world of ambigrams called to me. My heart filled with a whole new melody, one of mirrored symmetry, of yin and yang symbology, and of typographic symphony.

Ambigram lettering is a graphic designer's most poetic language. Like every art form, it begins by synthesizing intangible and seemingly disconnected messages into an original concept. Successful ambigrams uncover intriguing characters and express emotional themes, resulting in a memorable story. They also echo harmony and melody through each curve and syncopated serif, creating a rhythmic musicality. The designer then translates and crafts the concept, story, and musicality into an aesthetically beautiful composition. And by the sweep of the pencil and the plotting of pixels, visual poetry is played out on the page.

CONCEPT

One of the most incredible rewards of being human is that every one of us is a natural creator. We're born with the tools and curiosity to explore the path of our imagination—a mind to analyze, senses to experience, emotions to feel, and time to choose what we make of ourselves.

Ambigrams, born from the seed of ideation, are malleable, disconnected fragments that the graphic designer fuses into a one-of-a-kind fingerprint. Discovering these pieces requires focused time, attention, and nourishment. We don't like to admit it, but generating these ideas can often bring frustration and an ache that taunts and lures us into further exploring, creating, and growing. For anyone who has raised kids, the early stages are much like the terrible twos—temper tantrums, short attention span, and loss of patience. But the process also inspires an adventurous spirit, a raw connection to emotion, a sense of presence, and an eagerness to learn. Fortunately, the design of our brain helps us move past those initial growing pains. Our analytical, message-driven left brain and our wildly inventive, emotional right brain work in sync to see the big picture as well as its details, the forest and the trees, and the letterforms and their poetic symmetry. This internal creative eye connects related and, more often, unrelated events and objects. And when this vision manifests on the page, it becomes a concept.

Ambigrams are an adventure in discovery. Hidden between serifs and ligatures is a secret language where shape takes meaning and form meets function. Taking a look at the mirrored Paris ambigram in *Figure 1.1*, it's an excellent example of an unexpected discovery emerging from the flanking curves of the P and S. Through the synthesis of the Eiffel Tower graphic and the letterforms, the concept takes on its meaning.

Figure 1.1 The architectural balance and symmetry of the Eiffel Tower mimicked by the letterforms allows word and graphic to fuse into a single clear concept. (Nikita Prokhorov)

STORY

Brilliant writers invent a story by weaving pen and ink through their imagination. Engaging speakers invite us into a personal story through their passionate voice and persuasive presence. And innovative filmmakers orchestrate fantastic journeys through sights, sounds, and emotional performances. Words create worlds. Pictures ignite emotion. Heroes conquer villains. Resistance fights persistence. Truth meets conflict. These are the bones of a great story.

Robert McKee, author of the screenwriter's bible *Story* (ReganBooks, 1997) believes "stories are metaphors for life." A story is a synthesis of message, meaning, and metamorphosis through a hero's crisis, choices, and changes. Stories need characters, a setting, mood, and genre. Most of all, a story needs a great storyteller—a voice to carry the audience across the peaks and valleys through crisis and triumph, and create a "believable" world. The storyteller shares a message to our mind, evokes emotions in our hearts, and delivers meaning through the content.

The graphic designer naturally embraces the role of storyteller.

EMOTIONAL CONNECTION

Human beings thrive on emotion, and our intuitive minds operate on it. We thirst for it like water in the desert. We hunger for it like popcorn in the theater. We long for it like a kiss from our lover. We crave it like chocolate; OK, maybe chocolate isn't everyone's choice. But emotion is the fuel that inspires curiosity, evokes desires, and drives action. The designer's role is to evoke an emotional response through his knowledge of design principles and deliberate aesthetic choices. The designer's insight into color theory, for example, means he knows choosing red will infer passion (*Figure 1.2*), desire, and action, whereas cool blue tones will elicit a sense of peace, serenity, and stability. Curvelinear forms usually harken softer, "feminine" emotions of open-mindedness, friendliness, and joy. And with angular shapes, the audience will

THE DESIGNER'S ROLE IS TO EVOKE AN EMOTIONAL RESPONSE THROUGH HIS KNOWLEDGE OF DESIGN PRINCIPLES AND DELIBERATE AESTHETIC CHOICES.

Figure 1.2 The color and imagery shown in this ambigram allude to passion and love, and connect with the viewer on visual and emotional levels.

Figure 1.3 Jagged, triangular shapes and a high-contrast palette evoke aggression and fear in this highly detailed ambigram. (Mark Palmer)

sense closed-mindedness, and deliberate and aggressive emotions. Use of common symbols often drives the emotional connection more directly. Hearts, for example, the irrefutable symbol for love, can quickly shift the emotional radar toward longing or endearment. Whereas repeated triangular shapes will infer the jagged edge of danger and shift emotional triggers to aggression and fear (*Figure 1.3*).

ARCHETYPOGRAPHY

Character archetypes have been threaded through mythology and psychology for millennia. Defined as the ideal model of a person, personality, or behavior, Plato began articulating archetypes with his "form theory" and the notion of an orderly universe. Greek mythology made attempts, through gods and goddesses, to explain the origins of the world. Swiss psychiatrist and psychologist Carl Jung first used the term "archetype" to describe his work in "collective unconscious" and define universal behavior patterns

Figure 1.4 The blackletter here is masculine, purposeful, and stoic. (Elwin Gill)

Figure 1.5 The lyrical approach to this lettering evokes elegance and romance, a perfect choice to represent the union of man and wife in matrimony. (Andy Martin)

in all stories. And Joseph Campbell's comparative mythology expanded on Jung's approach to create even more specific character models, including The Hero, The Mentor, and The Trickster.

In the language of graphic design, these archetypes are otherwise known as gothic, blackletter, display, script, traditional, modern, and more. Designers well versed in their craft recognize that the personality traits behind each of these letterform families are based on culture, historical movement, and media. When creating a new typographic statement, designers make choices based on this insight. The blackletter becomes the masculine, purposeful, stoic lettering design as in the Trick or Treat ambigram in *Figure 1.4*, and a feminine, curvilinear, lyrical direction is represented by the more freeform script in the Peter N Sarah ambigram in *Figure 1.5*. Understanding and applying character "archetypography" helps designers create unique personality types.

MUSICALITY

• **Composition.** In music, composition is the underlying structure that unifies an orchestral score. It's a balance of harmony with melody and contrast of dissonance with consonance. A graphic designer composes in much the same manner. He visualizes the complete piece in his mind's eye but knows the role each color, line, weight, and texture will play in the final performance. In typographic design an overarching melody can carry the eye through the letters via consistent weight distribution and repeated motifs. The overall shape of the lettering design will also influence how the viewer interprets the meaning and emotion. Is it more structured and rhythmic as in the Menagerie ambigram in *Figure 1.6* or is it more free-flowing and lyrical as in the Rock 'n' Roll ambigram in *Figure 1.7*? The designer infuses a variety of "instruments" into his composition, including glyphs, ligatures, swashes, and other ornamentation. Variations in color, texture, and weight add visual dynamics to build an even fuller performance.

Figure 1.6 Menagerie. (Cheryl Savala, Menagerie Creative)

Figure 1.7 Rock 'n' Roll. (Kai Hammond)

Each of these ambigrams dances to the beat of a different drummer. Menagerie is a syncopated, structured march, whereas Rock 'n' Roll is more improvisational and lyrical.

Figure 1.8 This ambigram has it all: emotional connectivity, heroic archetypography, balanced composition, and a visually stunning aesthetic. (Bastian Pinnenberg)

MOOD

Memorable musical compositions immediately set a mood through key, tempo, and timbre. The haunting bassoon "da dum, da dum" in the score for *Jaws* is more foreboding in its minor key than the triumphant major key fanfare of *Star Wars*. The designer realizes that every choice creates this specific tonal language. In movie marketing this is referred to as genre— romance, action adventure, comedy, fantasy—and each contains its own visual language. The Ringworld ambigram in *Figure 1.8* is an ideal example of combining a beautifully balanced composition with heroic archetypography and an aesthetically stunning rendering to show fantasy, magic, and intrigue.

Figure 1.9 Charmed. (Nikita Prokhorov)

Figure 1.10 Elite. (Johan Skylling)

Each of these designs embodies the most critical characteristic of a successful ambigram—strong legibility unimpeded by the design.

CRAFT

Without question, the most significant challenge facing the ambigram designer is to create solutions that read in full clarity. Legibility simply cannot be sacrificed for symmetry, aesthetic style, or personal ego. The most successful solutions are uncomplicated, unencumbered, and uncompromised. When concept, story, and musicality fuse, the final step is for the designer to call upon his most critical eye and talented hand to carve away at the final details. He pays meticulous attention to every cut, curve, and corner using only the most precise tools. Whether a marker on cardboard or a highly polished CG rendering, the final presentation will embody every creative choice made along the creative journey (*Figures 1.9.* and *1.10*).

It's been a privilege to review the stunning collection of work on the pages that follow. This infectious passion for "poetic lettering" crosses countries and cultures, and I salute the adventurous designers who brave the world of ambigram and in turn inspire artists across the globe.

In addition to those you've just heard from, several other designers served as judges for this project and offer commentary in the following Case Studies section. Here's more about them.

SCOT MORRIS

Scot Morris has a B.A from DePauw University and a Ph.D. in Clinical Psychology from Southern Illinois University. He was the Associate Editor of *Psychology Today* and a founding editor (later, Senior Editor and "Games" editor) for *OMNI* magazine. He introduced Scott Kim to the world in his "Games Column." The magazine ran a competition based on that column, and it elicited several hundred original ambigrams. His writing appeared in *OMNI*, *Psychology Today*, *Penthouse*, *Playboy*, *Family Weekly*, *Architectural Digest*, and *Golf*. His photography has appeared in *Penthouse*, *Time*, *Newsweek*, *Scientific American*, *Family Weekly*, *Architectural Digest*, *Golf*, *Stern*, *Panorama*, *Paris Match*, *Games*, and *TV Guide*.

STEFAN G. BUCHER

Stefan G. Bucher is the man behind 344design.com and the popular online drawing and story-telling experiment dailymonster.com. He is the author of the books *100 Days of Monsters*, *All Access*, *The Graphic Eye*, *You Deserve a Medal—Honors on the Path to True Love*, *344 Questions—The Creative Person's Do-It-Yourself Guide to Insight, Survival, and Artistic Fulfillment*, and *The Yeti Story*, which he wrote and illustrated exclusively for Saks Fifth Avenue. He has created designs for David Hockney, Judd Apatow, and The New York Times. D&AD honored him with a Yellow Pencil for book design, and the Art Directors Club of New York declared him a Young Gun back in 2004. He designed the titles for the motion pictures *The Fall*, *Immortals*, and *Mirror, Mirror* by director Tarsem, and his time-lapse drawings appear on the Emmy-award winning TV show *The Electric Company* on PBS.

JESSICA HISCHE

Jessica Hische is a letterer, illustrator, and self-described "avid internetter." After graduating with a degree in Graphic and Interactive Design from Tyler School of Art (Temple University) in 2006, she worked for Headcase Design in Philadelphia before taking a position as Senior Designer at Louise Fili Ltd. While working for Louise, she learned most of her skills as a letterer and spent upwards of 16 hours every day working (9 for Louise, 7+ for freelance clients). After two and a half years, Jessica left to further her freelance career and embark on several fun personal projects. Jessica began Daily Drop Cap, a project in which every day she created a new illustrative letter, working through the alphabet a total of 12 times. At its peak, the site had more than 100,000 visitors per month. It culminated with a thirteenth alphabet, each letter crafted by a guest contributor. Jessica has become as well known for her side projects as she has for her client work. Although she doesn't consider herself a web designer, many of her personal projects are web-centric. She's created several educational microsites, including Mom This Is How Twitter Works, Should I Work for Free?, and Don't Fear the Internet (with Russ Maschmeyer), each as entertaining as they are helpful. She coined the term "procrastiworking" to describe her tendency to procrastinate on client work by working on personal projects.

Jessica's clients include Wes Anderson, Tiffany & Co., The New York Times, Penguin Books, Target, Leo Burnett, American Express, and Wired Magazine. She has also released several commercial typefaces, which are available in her store. Jessica has been named a Print Magazine New Visual Artist (20 under 30), one of Forbes, 30 under 30 in Art and Design, an ADC Young Gun, a "Person to Watch" by GD USA, and one of 25 Emerging Artists by STEP Magazine. She's been personally profiled in many magazines, including *Eye Magazine* (UK), *Communication Arts*, *Grafik Magazine* (UK), and *Novum Magazine* (Germany). She is currently serving on the Type Directors Club Board of Directors and divides her time fairly evenly between San Francisco, Brooklyn, and airports en route to design and illustration conferences.

CHAPTER 2
CASE STUDIES

John Langdon

SYZYGY

AN ALIGNMENT
OF 3 HEAVENLY
BODIES OF THE
SOLAR SYSTEM.

THE JOINING OF
TWO ENTITIES,
WITHOUT LOSS
OF IDENTITIES.

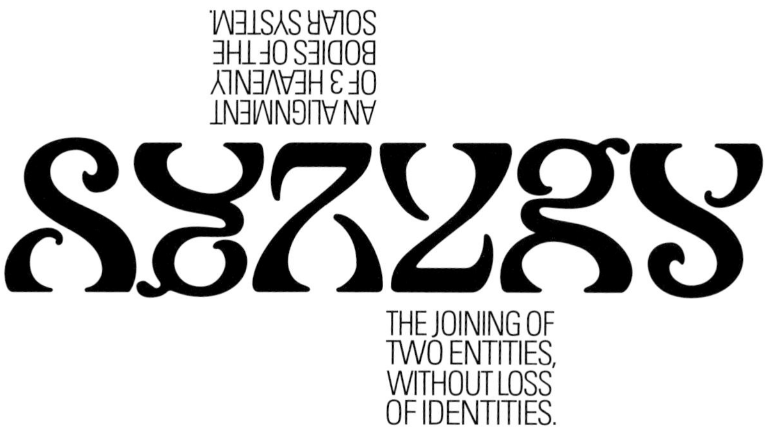

Figure 2.1 The finished ambigram.

I first heard the word "syzygy" on Cheers in the mid 1980s. Fans of the show might recall that it was the name of Diane Chambers's poetry group. Something told me it was a pretty cool word, and a few years later, it turned out to fit nicely into my book of ambigrams called Wordplay. In those days, before the Internet had become popular and before Dan Brown had written his first book, I chose the words I designed as ambigrams based on their meanings. Most of the words that interested me were words that denoted or implied some duality that I could relate to my primary influence and inspiration—the yin and yang symbol—and especially those that also had some relevance in Western physics. Hence, "syzygy" was a winner.

As I always do, I began by writing the word upside down. Briefly studying each letter, I try to envision it as if it were its counterpart facing in the opposite direction: The last letter of the inverted word (farthest to the left) corresponds to the first letter of the word right-side up. In other words, I try to envision something that's the same as, yet distinctly different from,

what I'm actually seeing. In the case of the word SYZYGY, I had a very unusual group of letters—the rhythmic repetition of three Ys—and each had to appear as a different letter when viewed from the opposite point of view. While looking at my early explorations (*Figures 2.2a, 2.2b, 2.2c, 2.2d*), I seem to have assumed that I would never be able to invert a G into a Y, and that therefore I would have to build the first Y out of parts of the letters on either side. I was getting somewhere with the G, I think, but I was simultaneously forcing myself to create a Y/Y (*Figures 2.2b, 2.2c*). Apparently, those Ys convinced me to start over. In fact, studies have shown that we read the tops of letters more than the bottoms, which is a critically important aspect of ambigram design because it allows a doubly directional glyph to have two "tops"—one facing each way. In extreme situations, I can even eliminate parts of the bottom of a letter, knowing/hoping that the top will identify it sufficiently. Note that Ys, by definition, are always open at the top. Therefore, the bottoms of the S, Z, and G would all have to be open (see the orange circles). I'm

Figure 2.2 Initial sketches.

Figure 2.3 Detailed pencil sketch.

guessing that the seemingly extraneous AIGA ambigram had something to do with deciding that an open-bottomed G would still read as a G. The green circles indicate places where the S and Z needed to appear open to read those two letters, and they

needed to appear closed when they were supposed to read as Ys.

So with a new start (*Figure 2.2e, 2.2f, 2.2g*) I began working on a one-letter-to-one-letter exchange and clearly structured the letters. But I wasn't in love with the G/Y glyph, so I tried a lowercase G form (*Figure 2.2h*) and liked that better. Then I began developing some style, putting some meat on the bones (*Figure 2.2i*). The S/Y and the Z/Y glyphs had places that needed to connect (for the Ys, see the green circles) and be separate (for the S and the Z). In these situations, I bring the parts that need to be joined closer together than they normally would be, but still keep them separate. This situation also helps me make a couple of stylistic decisions: (1) the letter style will be thick and thin, allowing me to emphasize critically important and defining parts of the letter, and diminish the notice-ability of difficult areas, and (2) strokes will end with soft, rounded terminals, which is a subtlety that allows part of the rounded area (top of the Z serif) to be close to the part it would be connected to for the Y, but the rest of that rounded terminal pulls away.

The symmetry of the (inverted) G (*Figure 2.2i*) didn't work for me because it didn't relate well to the more organic forms of the S and Z, so I changed it to a more conventional form (*Figure 2.2j*). This also helped the tops of all the Ys to look very similar. I enlarged sketch 9 significantly to trace over it for my finished drawing (*Figure 2.1*) in which I made many subtle adjust-ments and refinements. The letter height in the drawing in *Figure 2.3* is about 1.5 inches. Normally, I would have transferred the final drawing to paper (in those pre-Adobe Illustrator days), but in this case the finished art (*Figure 2.1*) was done on acetate laid over the finished drawing to save time. Years later, I scanned the finished drawing and redid it in Illustrator.

CHERYL SAVALA John's study in simplification and stylization of form in SYZYGY is masterful. Although the word is very uncommon, each letter is immediately recognizable and legible.

JESSICA HISCHE Syzygy is definitely a tough word to begin with, but it's such a wonderfully appropriate word for an ambigram! I love the style of lettering. It has a wonderful rhythm, and I particularly like the Y/G flip, even though the Y is a bit wild. I think the S/Y is a bit of a stretch, but because it mimics the shape of the Y in the Y/G combination, it holds together nicely. Only John could make such a strange word so instantly legible in ambigram form.

SCOT MORRIS I like the challenge of three types of Ys in the word. John is handicapped by the fact that most people don't know the word. I asked a friend to decipher the word, and she came up with SYZYGS—pretty close.

SCOTT KIM John Langdon creates ambigrams at the deepest artistic level, choosing words resonant with dual meanings and holding his ambigrams to the same standards of legibility as his professional, graphic design work. Here we see John tackle a particularly difficult subject. "Syzygy" is an uncommon word with an unusual letter pattern that requires three different interpretations of the same letter, Y. Notice how the style of the lettering—thin and thick with rounded ends and curly flourishes—is not imposed from the outside. The style emerges organically as a way to make the letters legible and harmonious.

STEFAN G. BUCHER Cropping the bottom of the letters to achieve other glyphs on the turn is a very clever idea that yields a great graphic look for the final ambigram. Although I love learning a new word—particularly one as cool as syzygy—its obscurity hampers the ambigram. It might be worthwhile to add the word SYZYGY to the explanatory type blocks to let people know they've decoded the ambigram correctly. Either that or get the piece published in a magazine for crossword and Scrabble aficionados.

NIKITA PROKHOROV John takes a word that is difficult to spell and to pronounce... and makes a true masterpiece out of it. Beautiful consistency of the letterforms, especially when you consider three different letter combinations for the letter Y.

Figure 2.1 The finished ambigram.

I created the history ambigram specifically for the book Ambigrams Revealed. The word was chosen based on its importance, simplicity, and content. It's a word that encompasses many themes or all of them, because everything has its history.

To create this ambigram, I didn't need many drafts: It is a relatively easy word, has almost natural combinations, such as h/y and i/r, and the letter t is the central letter (*Figure 2.2*). The greatest difficulty was the s/o combination. However, in the past I created other ambigrams that utilized that letter flip, and because I had some previous versions to build on, it was not as big a challenge as anticipated (*Figure 2.3*).

Most of my ambigrams are developed with sketches using paper and pencil first. Then they are redrawn on the computer using Corel Draw. Because "history" turned out to be a fairly simple ambigram, I could get away with using an existing typeface and modifying it to achieve the desired objective. After the sketches were completed, I chose a typeface that matched the style I was going for. The condensed typeface Onyx, originally developed in the late 1930s by American Type Founders, provided a beautiful base of a contrasted design and a bold page presence.

To make the ambigram appear more compact, I decreased the stem of the h. Although that may have compromised the legibility a bit, the overall aesthetic of the ambigram wasn't affected much. Sometimes we have to choose between the design and readability, and in this case, I struck a good balance between both.

Figure 2.2 Initial sketch.

Figure 2.3 Detailed sketch.

STEP-BY-STEP DIGITAL TRANSFORMATION

Step 1 The word "history" is set in the Onyx typeface.

Step 2 The leg of the h is shortened and the i is removed and replaced by the upside-down r.

Step 3 The terminal of the f is used for the h to mimic the tail of the y when the h is upside down. It closely resembles the original tail of the y, yet works better with the rigid vertical of the h.

Step 4 The bottom of the t is removed and replaced with a duplicate of the top of the t. Because it is the central letter, it needs to appear the same regardless of how the ambigram is viewed.

Step 5 The original o is modified slightly to look like an s when rotated 180 degrees. Although it is a custom letter and because it was created using original glyphs from the Onyx typeface, it still fits in stylistically with the rest of the ambigram.

Step 6 The serifs of the letters are all altered to give them a smoother and more rounded appearance.

before

after

Step 7 Subtle highlights are added to complete the ambigram.

CHERYL SAVALA What makes this solution so strong for me is evident in the details: The modification of the serifs, the balance/counterbalance through kerning, and the additional inline adds a nice sophisticated touch to move it beyond a font manipulation.

JESSICA HISCHE This is a very easy read, and I love the general style of lettering. My only feedback would be to keep the terminals a bit more consistently shaped. The ball terminal on the y/h combo is a lot rounder than the very teardrop-shaped terminal on the r/i. Overall though, great sample, good vector curves, and I love the highlight detail.

JOHN LANGDON This successful and pleasing ambigram owes much to the selection of a cooperative word, an intelligent choice of styles, and an excellent manipulation/management of the one really challenging glyph: the o/s. The condensed proportion of the style allows the distinctive features of the S to be "hidden" very low on the O. The hi/ry presented the designer with a difficult choice: significantly alter the structure of the h and y or introduce a kerning problem. The beauty of the word as a whole is retained with this solution at the expense of the structure of two letters.

SCOT MORRIS A very legible rendering of a word that seems relatively easy to do. The analysis of how to work within a particular font is quite instructive.

SCOTT KIM Here we see an ambigram produced by surgically altering an existing typeface. Only words that work easily as ambigrams are candidates for this sort of operation. Most ambigrams require much more unusual letter shapes. As Cleber Faria notes, legibility suffers a bit in the quest to achieve regular visual rhythm: The kerned H and I make for even spacing between the vertical strokes of the letters but make for an awkward Y. The alternative would be to let the right foot of the H touch the ground, but this would open up an awkward gap between the H and I to make room for the ear of the R.

STEFAN G. BUCHER Scavenging the terminal of the lowercase f is a stylish move and nicely mirrors the i/r combination. (Personally, I'd have placed it a bit higher on the h to avoid the slightly awkward bump going into the shoulder of the h. I might have lowered the dot over the i, too, to make the whole shape even more compact, but it's a great clear ambigram.)

NIKITA PROKHOROV Although seemingly an easy word, the O/S flip is a challenging combination, and Cleber makes it look very natural. The H may seem a little awkward due to the height difference in vertical strokes, but it doesn't take away from the impeccable attention to the details or the legibility of the word.

Figure 2.1 Finished ambigram.

For the case study, I selected the word "wishmaster." I have always looked for the extraordinary and remarkable words for my ambigrams, and wishmaster was a perfect fit because it had a bit of magic and mystery. I perceive ambigrams as the secret codes. Therefore, I never use everyday, ordinary words for my ambigrams.

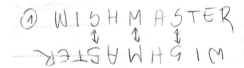

Figure 2.2 Initial sketch.

I first analyzed the arrangement of the letters in the word, and then I grouped them in the following pairs: W/ER, I/T, and H/S. The remaining letters, S and M, are naturally the same when they are rotated (*Figure 2.2*). The presence of pairings that work well together, as well as letters that read the same upside down, affects and enhances the readability of the ambigram.

Figure 2.3 Blackletter style exploration.

The first sketch I make is usually in the blackletter style (*Figure 2.3*). My early ambigrams, inspired by John Langdon's artwork, were frequently drawn in that style. To this day, a quick blackletter sketch reveals the "ambigrammatic potential" of the word.

Figure 2.4 More early sketches for the "wishmaster" ambigram.

Because decorative script is my favorite style, I decided to render this ambigram in that style (*Figure 2.5*). The initial quick sketches helped explore the potential connections between the letters. After most of the connections were determined, I improved each connection by increasing the weight of each letter and tightening the aesthetic of the word (*Figure 2.6a*). The sketch in *Figure 2.6b* was the last one; it roughly defines the base of the vector shape for each letter. My handmade sketches are usually inaccurate because all the subtleties and refinements are made on the computer.

Figure 2.5 Script style exploration.

Figure 2.6a Detailed script sketch.

Figure 2.6b Start of the vector drawing process.

CHERYL SAVALA Interlocking script lettering is one of the most difficult solutions for an ambigram, but when it works as well as it does here, it raises the bar of excellence. The transformation of the WI into TER demonstrates Daniel's talent for lettering, and his decision to add an inline brings an extra finesse and threads the entire piece together beautifully.

JESSICA HISCHE I love the flow of this ambigram. Although it references blackletter, it doesn't feel as stiff or forced as some blackletter ambigrams can. The curves could be tidied up, mostly the swash that makes up the top of the T/bottom of the I, which feels like it has a bit of flatness in some parts. I'd also adjust the white space in the H/A flip, which feels more open than the rest of the word. The WIS/STER flip is impressive—love how it's handled!

JOHN LANGDON It seems possible that untrained eyes might have difficulty reading this ambigram. Although it is gorgeous to behold and admirable in the creativity of the glyph solutions—most notably the W/er—the musical virtuosity of the style may be in conflict to some degree with the readability. Specifically, the W/er has been unnecessarily complicated by decorative flourishes (the central horizontal of the W/e and the extension of the bottom of the s/top of the T). Although beautiful, they add bits of complexity in the most complicated, and difficult to decipher, locations.

MAGGIE MACNAB What I like most about this ambigram is its fluid hand lettering, which the designer evolved from the original blacklettering calligraphic style. It is appropriate to both the meaning and the physical characters of the word. There is a bit of a pileup in the W beginning and ER ending, but the graceful execution of the letters help to save it. Ambigrams are meant to be brain twisters in many cases, and part of the fun is figuring them out.

SCOTT KIM Although I enjoy the fluid flow of flourishes in the final ambigram, the more angular blackletter style in Figure 2.3 would have resulted in better legibility, especially because the t and e would have stayed in lowercase and been consistent with (most of) the other letters. Notice how the continued lines of the flourishes allow the lowercase h to turn into a lowercase a—a difficult combination to pull off.

STEFAN G. BUCHER This ambigram is clear and beautiful all the way through "Wishma" and then gets lost a bit in the last four letters. The first part is so clear that I notice my confusion at the end more than I otherwise would. The solution may be to complicate the center of the ambigram to balance the decoding speed.

NIKITA PROKHOROV Wishmaster is a very complex word that's beautifully rendered. The simplicty of the hma competes with the complexity of the wis/ster, but in context they work very well together. Maybe fewer flourishes within the wis/ster combination would help balance out the word a little bit more.

Figure 2.1 The finished ambigram with the shading and details.

The city of San Diego in the southwestern corner of California is where I keep my heart and soul. Twice in my career in the United States Navy I was stationed here, and both times I loved every minute. My daughters are definitely Southern California girls.

I'm sure a few followers of ambigrams and my work have seen the other version of my San Diego design. Let me give you a little background of how it came to be. I was in a meeting at work, not paying attention and doodling as usual on some yellow lined paper. That doodle would evolve and later take second place in one of the original Ambigram Challenges on Ambigram.com. Like many designers, I started designing ambigrams after seeing John Langdon's work in *Angels & Demons* by Dan Brown.

In the Ambigram.com challenge, I took second place behind John, which was quite an honor for me. So with all that in mind, a remake of one of my favorite designs just seemed to make sense. The newer version of the design is much larger and more detailed. I also made some changes along the way to add to the overall aesthetic. In addition, I took out the 619 in this design, but I did love the fact that the area code is a natural ambigram all on its own.

When I started reworking this design, I first took a step back and looked at the original. I thought about what I wanted to change and what I wanted to keep. I knew that I wanted the D in the middle to remain more or less how it was, but the S/O solution could be improved. I'm a big fan of lettering and typography, and my background

Figure 2.2 Initial sketch.

in drafting (in high school and in college) gave me some of the tools I use today to create my ambigrams. Fortunately, I knew the solution to this design prior to starting, but for discussion purposes, I'll share one of the thought processes I use when I'm designing ambigrams. I've reached a point that when I look at any word, I can come up with some sort of solution that relies on the number of vertical strokes in the word or words. By that I mean if you can match up the number of vertical strokes between the words "San Diego" for example, you can find your solution. I used the D in Diego as my center point, but there are three letters in front of it and four letters after it, so the solution required me to figure out how to match up the number of vertical strokes in each letter.

Unless I am doodling, I usually start with guidelines for the top and bottom of the letters and some lines in between, which are properly spaced to assist with the placement of other parts of the letters (*Figure 2.2*). If you have formal typography training, I'm sure you know all the proper terminology to use for these lines, but I don't, so please forgive me. This may sound a bit unusual, but when I start almost any of my designs, I have no idea how they will look when they are completed. Often, I don't even know I am done until I feel like I have run out of more to do.

In this design, I knew that I wanted there to be more lines and curves, and I wanted an old-school tattoo look to it because that is a big part of the San Diego culture that I love. With this design, I drew out the first half of the design with all of its guidelines and errors on my drafting table. Once I thought that the design was good enough to continue, I moved on to my trusty light table that I built for my tattoo designs. This allowed me to trace the two sides of the design with more precision, creating a much more refined final piece. After I had all the letters drawn, the accents were all that were left to do. This is when I felt the nerves kick in a little (*Figure 2.3*). All the work I had done to that point could be ruined if one of my curves was not exactly like the other. I honestly wanted this design to be done completely freehand, so I didn't use any of my French curves or circle templates that I would normally use, which really brought out a quality in the end design that you don't get from ambigrams created digitally. That is not to say that I don't love computer-generated designs. I do, and once I am more proficient in the use of drawing software, I will draw more ambigrams digitally. However, my passion will always be handmade designs.

As I mentioned earlier, I never really know when my design is final. In fact, I wouldn't be surprised if over the next few days I add a line here or a curve there. But for submission to this book, I'm very pleased with what I created and look forward to seeing all the designs. Most likely, I'll frame the original print and hang it at home. Admittedly, I've wanted to take this ambigram for a spin for quite some time, and now that I have, I am happy to share it with you.

Figure 2.3 Outline sketch of the entire ambigram.

JUDGE'S COMMENTS

CHERYL SAVALA A beautiful design incorporating blacklettering and ornamentation. The high-contrast nature of the teardrop filigree detracts a bit from the lettering legibility. A solid fill to the letterforms and more closure on the d would enhance the readability.

JESSICA HISCHE This one is a very difficult read. I had to read through the creator's notes to realize what the word was. I keep wanting to make the S/O flip that the artist intended into an S/G because of the swash that makes up the top of the S. I do like how the additional ornamentation is treated, and although there is a lot going on, it doesn't distract from the letterforms.

JOHN LANGDON My favorite image of this ambigram is Figure 2.3—taking in the exquisite drawing and decoration before the problems set in. I was unable to read this ambigram until I found "San Diego" in the artist's write-up. The fatal problem is the D. Without being able to decipher that letter, I became unsure if the third letter was an n or possibly an m followed by a lowercase l. The inconsistent spacing of the letters (large space between the a and the n; tiny space between the n and the D) is a lesser problem, but one that may have exacerbated the difficulty with reading the n and D.

SCOTT KIM Every ambigram artist needs to decide how to balance the conflicting needs of legibility and visual style. Here, Elwin Gill embraces borderline illegibility as part of the counterculture aesthetic of tattoos, loading up his design with elaborate flourishes. The result is a secret message—hard to read at first, but easy to decipher once you know what it says.

STEFAN G. BUCHER I had to cheat and read Elwin's description to figure this one out, but that takes little away from this delightful piece. I like the asymmetrical ornamentation and love that it's an actual drawing. Leaving the letters gray was a good move. It keeps the letters hidden among the vines, which adds to the mystery.

NIKITA PROKHOROV Elwin's background in calligraphy shines through in this piece. Although slightly difficult to read at first, that is not the nature of graffiti art. There is a nice balance between the letters and the decorative flourishes. Some of the letters are easier to recognize than others, and that helps fill in the gaps between the slightly more challenging letters, eventually leading to recognition of the whole word.

Figure 2.1 The finished ambigram.

From start to finish, this SharkAttack ambigram is one of my favorite ambigrams I've ever drawn. I created it for an international ambigram challenge, and the spirit of friendly competition seems to always brings out my best work. At the time, I was designing custom ambigram tattoos on a regular basis and because of time constraints I rarely had the opportunity to experiment. This challenge seemed like the perfect forum to do that.

The process started with simply writing the proposed text on a blank sheet of paper. Even though this particular challenge requested that artists attempt different types of ambigrams, as soon as I saw the words I immediately knew that I wanted to draw a traditional rotational ambigram. But first I needed to explore whether or not the two words would work asymmetrically (Shark/ Attack) or if a symmetrical (SharkAttack/ SharkAttack) solution would be better.

So, I started mentally evaluating the text to see if Shark would invert cleanly into Attack. It did. Once I locked down the best

solution in my head, I began to sketch the solution for the asymmetrical design: S–k, ha–tac, r–t, k–A (*Figure 2.2*). The solution worked out nicely, and I added some flare to disguise the top of the S, the terminal endings on the upstrokes in the k's, and the crossbars on the A's.

After studying the asymmetrical solution, I came to a realization: Although asymmetrical ambigrams are super impressive, it just didn't seem to fit well with the phrase "Shark Attack." When a hungry shark comes at you in open water, he's gonna "SharkAttack" all at once. An ambigram for Shark Attack definitely needed to convey the abrupt aggressiveness of a not-so-polite Great White. It needed to be instantly legible as an entire phrase, as well as stylistically aggressive and pointy. Now, this could have been achieved by simply duplicating the asymmetrical solution, inverting it, and shoving the Attack side into the end of the Shark side. But that wasn't good enough for me. The possibility of a longer symmetrical ambigram meant that I still had more solution exploring to do.

I really liked the S–k, ha–tac solution at the beginning of the asymmetrical design and wanted to keep that. So, in my head I kicked the single vertical r from the asymmetrical solution into a double vertical R to shift the A in Attack one vertical over to join the phrase as one and create that really cool RkAt–RkAt glyph in the middle. After I locked it down in my head, I drew it up. After I drew it up, I loved it.

However, the love was short-lived. After studying the new symmetrical solution, I noticed that I had almost all capital letters within the body of the phrase. I wanted the speed and aggressiveness of the two separate words joined in the middle by the shared vertical in the new symmetrical solution, but I really needed to save capital letters for the initial letter of each word. Doing so would create context and establish the clear legibility of the two-word phrase.

That meant the dual vertical capital R needed to go back to a single vertical lowercase r. Also, in order to retain the joining of the two words by a shared vertical, it meant that I had to somehow shave a vertical stroke off somewhere else in the beginning of the solution. I puzzled this issue for a few minutes, and that's when the solution to a previous tattoo design that I had recently drawn for a client surfaced in my memory. When drawn correctly, the natural curvature of an S is perfect for the second stroke in a k, and it would allow me to shave that pesky vertical stroke off the front of the solution that I needed to keep the words cleanly joined by a shared vertical. In the sketches, you can clearly see the single glyph at the top: Sh–ck. At this point, I could practically smell the blood in the water.

In an ambigram, the first and last letters are the most important for establishing clear legibility. So, I wanted to make sure

Figure 2.2 Initial sketches.

that the curvature of the initial S would invert as perfectly as possible into the final k. As I started to build the new solution around this notion, I realized that the c could now follow the almost natural shape of the second stroke in the h, and the new a–a combination made it much easier to keep it as lowercase. This was now followed by the lowercase r–t combo and the epic kAt–kAt glyph in the center to round out the shared vertical solution that I desired. This definitely felt like the solution for this ambigram.

Once I had the basic solution drawn up with some general direction for style, the final sketch didn't take long to complete. It's quite simply a larger, more detailed version of my initial drawings with some added style (*Figure 2.3*). I added other aggressive elements as well, like the spikes on the tops of the t's, the spines on the back of the final k, the diamond shapes through the middle of the ambigram, and the spines on the terminal endings of most letter strokes. However, my absolute favorite parts of this design are the shark bites in the outline at the beginning and the end. It's subtle thematic details like these that I love to sneak

Figure 2.3 Detailed sketch.

into ambigrams; they just add to the context of the piece as a whole.

Finally, I scanned the sketch into the computer, vector traced the design in Adobe Illustrator, and added a bit of a color and dimensional treatment for a final touch of style (*Figure 2.1*).

My goal throughout the project was to create an aggressively styled, clearly legible, and thematically consistent ambigram. The result is one of my favorite ambigrams, and I hope you enjoy it as much as I enjoyed creating it!

CHERYL SAVALA This is one of those ambigrams that's a complete knockout on all levels. First and foremost, it's easily legible. The conceptual approach to the lettering is original and evokes emotion and story, and the execution is quite sharp. Well done, Mark!

JESSICA HISCHE What a great phrase to ambigramify! I also love the artist's use of shark attack as a verb, which put a smile on my face. The lettering style is great for the subject, and I love the use of bifurcation and the little spurs along the center line. It's incredibly legible and has a really good rhythm. This artwork is destined for a t-shirt; it makes me want to form a metal band if only to use this ambigram as the band logo!

JOHN LANGDON This ambigram is very successful. It reads quickly and easily, as I suspect it would even without the exuberant imagery. Unlike other submissions that employ lavish decoration, this one is based on smart decisions, creating strong and highly recognizable letterforms. Quibbles: the upper arm of the Ks (particularly the first one) are too heavy and thus a bit distracting. The "flag" of the r is too short and weakens that letter. It could easily have been handled like the overlapping connector of the two parts of the h. Given the sophistication of these letterforms, and the appropriate and well-integrated beveled-blade background, the serrations at either end seem silly.

SCOT MORRIS A quite legible rendering of SHARK ATTACK. My guest judge had no difficulty with it. Mark has done a nice job turning the SH into CK. I like the "aggressive elements" of the design—the points, the spines, and especially the shark's jaws.

SCOTT KIM This ambigram combines a highly stylized, appropriately aggressive appearance with high legibility—a remarkable feat. I'm especially tickled by the ascending diagonal that runs from the bottom of the first A to the top of the last A. The S to K transformation is particularly difficult to get right: Here the lettering style fully rationalizes the peculiar angles of the letters.

STEFAN G. BUCHER If Mark hasn't already trademarked this ambigram, sold it to a sportswear company, or started a band by the same name, he'd better jump on it. This is masterful! It's clearly legible, the aggressive personality matches the word, and the shark teeth are a stroke of genius!

NIKITA PROKHOROV This is a great example of how the style of a word is perfectly suited for the actual meaning. Even before you read the word (which is instantly legible by the way!), you get a sense of threat and feel that danger is near. Compare it to hearing the music from *Jaws*: Your hair instantly stands up on end, and you get goosebumps without even knowing what's in the water beneath you.

Figure 2.1 The finished ambigram.

My friend's dishwasher magnet inspired me to design an ambigram from the words dirty/clean. The black and white magnet resembles a stop sign with the word dirty written at the top and the word clean upside down at the bottom—a perfect combination and application for an ambigram. However, I was skeptical about the outcome of the d–n and y–c letter combinations. Fortunately, perseverance paid off, and I produced an attractive design.

The first step involved determining letter combinations, which took a little time. I followed the typical process of turning one word upside down and lining it atop the other word (*Figure 2.2*).The letter combinations became d–n, ir–ea, t–l, and y–c. The next step included fusing these combinations together.

The easy structures to determine were the t–l and r–e combinations. The t–l combination in a capitalized script style created a natural ambigram. For the r–e combination, a capital e can create the lobe and leg of a capital r, and have the e's top arm thin compared to the rest of the letter to minimize the disruption of legibility to the r.

I discovered that I could achieve the a shape by joining a lowercase i with the stem of the uppercase r because the lower part of the i naturally curves to the right. After making several attempts to solve the crossbar issue, I capitalized the i and added a swash to the top of the letter to create the crossbar. Next, I needed to find a new

Figure 2.2 Initial sketch.

Figure 2.3 Stylistic exploration.

Figure 2.4

solution to connect the i to the r because the bottom of a capitalized script style i curves to the left instead of the right (*Figure 2.3*). The issue was solved by extending the bottom of the stem of the r to the left, which surpassed the first attempt in making the a look natural.

Only two options seemed to exist for the y–c combination: to have the right diagonal stroke of the y come off the bottom part of the c or to extend the top stroke of the c back through the letter to the baseline. The first option offers no real reason for the y's stroke to be there, and the second option, which is the one I chose to go with, does provide a reason because it's attached naturally to the c.

The d–n combination proved to be the most difficult. I initially tried using a lowercase n, which made the bottom of the capital d look awkward. Because the capital letter d has a naturally straight stem and a smooth bowl, I ruled out the lowercase n because it interrupted those characteristics (*Figure 2.4*). Finding a usable solution for using a capital n seemed to be the way to go, plus it would keep all of the letters uppercase (*Figure 2.5*). After sketching out all of the possible variations, I chose the solution that met the criteria of keeping the stem of the d straight and the bowl a decent shape. The lower part of the d's stem curves to the left to resemble the same feel of the other letters and to prevent it from looking like a capital h. The top part of the bowl is thin, and the enclosure to the stem is suggestive for the n to be legible.

Throughout the structural process, I played with the letters' style; in fact, the letters usually tell me what style they want to be in. Because of the t–l and y–c combinations, the style was influenced by a script/ calligraphy type of style (*Figure 2.6*).

Figure 2.5 Uppercase letter exploration.

Figure 2.6 Detailed stylistic exploration.

The design was finished off with a background shape to encompass the words. Scroll ornaments were added to the inside top and bottom of the shape to fill in the empty space and to provide a base for the words to sit on. Although they are altered a bit, the ornaments are made from the y–c letter combination, which helps them be in harmony with the letters.

I kept the colors black and white for the contrast and the classiness. The overall design worked out well: A clear baseline exists, all letters are uppercase, the letter style is consistent, distracting strokes are minimal, and the words are legible.

CHERYL SAVALA Why haven't we seen this in retail stores? What a brilliant concept, and so practically inspired. It's not often that an all caps italic word can balance and read so easily, but Nicholas has certainly shown typography designers how to make it happen. The strokes flow nicely into one another, allowing the eye to carry through the word in either direction.

JESSICA HISCHE I love the idea of flipping this little sticker on my own dishwasher. The style is really nice, and I was surprised at how legible the C/Y combo is. Because the artist is already incorporating unattached swashes that are just there for decoration, I think that they could be pulled into the word area a little bit to even out the tiny white space issue of the area above the C/ below the Y. It looks great when you read DIRTY, but the word looks a tad bottom heavy as CLEAN. The E/R flip is handled really well too.

JOHN LANGDON This type of ambigram is sometimes called a "symbiotogram," meaning two different words with a well-established, integrated relationship—most often words with opposite meanings. Symmetry has inherent aesthetic appeal, and it's harder to create an attractive symbiotogram than a symmetrical ambigram. The symmetrical cartouche and flourishes help, but these letterforms are clean (yes!) and uncomplicated, resulting in an enjoyable and readable, if somewhat understated, ambigram. It would be improved with added space between the A–N/D–I.

MAGGIE MACNAB This ambigram is a little difficult to capture at first, but this is the case of many ambigrams, because you are looking at letterforms in a distorted configuration. It takes a moment to adjust your perceptions to what you are seeing, much like tuning your ear to a new dialect. You recognize the word in general terms, but the inflections appear awkward and strange until you learn them. Fortunately, we big-brained humans pick up on these sorts of things as a matter of course, and once deciphered, we quickly advance into the entirely new dimension of reading yet another word—the opposite of the first, rotated at 180 degrees. It is like figuring out a puzzle, which most find a very satisfying exercise.

SCOT MORRIS This is quite legible in a clever, practical design. His challenge of turning a C into a Y and an N into a D was dealt with successfully. I also like his observations about how the letters tell what style they want to be in.

SCOTT KIM A charmingly calligraphic solution to a classic ambigram challenge. Other similar practical ambigrammatic sign challenges include OPEN/CLOSED and PUSH/PULL.

STEFAN G. BUCHER Ha! Fun! Very nicely done! I love it. This also illustrates that the obvious difficulty of creating an ambigram lets you get away with design choices that would otherwise get you a slap to the back of the head. The word DIRTY feels very much like using a script face in ALL CAPS mode, which makes me foam at the mouth. But because it's happening in the service of a well-executed bit of graphic delight, I feel at peace.

Figure 2.1 The finished piece (top) and the Photoshop-generated duplicate to show the reflection (bottom).

Tempt is a fellow graffiti artist. He is a true king. Whether judged by quantity, quality, or range (temporal or stylistic), he qualifies in spades. And even beyond the esoteric qualifications of the graffiti community, he excels as a human being: He's smart, humble, funny, and more. But most important to me, Tempt is my good friend. Starting in 2003, he became disconnected from his physical graffiti tools—his hands and most of the rest of his voluntary muscles—by the paralyzing disease ALS. So when he emailed, "Personally I'd love to see a nice COSM silver fill and thick 3D like da old days, papi. Just sayin'," I was gratefully summoned out of retirement.

I've been creating ambigrams seriously for about 20 years, but this was my first attempt at fusing it with full-blown graffiti. The tag "Tempt" wasn't really a desperate challenge for a reflection ambigram: two terminal Ts and a central, inherently symmetrical M. But the freedom and verve of graffiti letterforms, and the art form's inherent treachery, allowed me to imbue the piece with mirror symmetry that was asymmetrical, a path I was enjoying exploring.

I worked up a couple of quick sketches (*Figure 2.2*) just to test the feasibility of the E/P reflection and stored the outline in my brain. The stars aligned when my paleoartist buddy Dennis Wilson offered me an

Figure 2.2 Initial sketches.

Figure 2.3 In-progress photos.

external wall of his studio in Denver. I was a bit rusty but dragged out the old skills to the best of my ability (*Figure 2.3*). Painting with spray paint certainly ain't Photoshop, so sharpness must be attained by more traditional drawing techniques, a bit of back and forth, and for an aging writer like me, patience (*Figure 2.4*). And drips of course, unless intentional, must be eradicated (*Figure 2.5*).

At the end of my trip out West, I visited Tempt in Los Angeles. It was my first time seeing him since he became sick, and I was able to deliver on his challenge (*Figure 2.1*). I showed him the finished ambigram piece on my camera and got his digital high five. His "voice" now emanates electronically from his computer, but the words are all his. Man, how things have changed.

Figure 2.4 Detailed letter work.

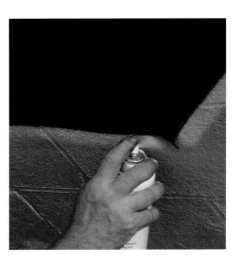

Figure 2.5 Touch-ups.

JUDGE'S COMMENTS

CHERYL SAVALA Such an incredible story behind the design. Inspired by friendship, love of street art, and lettering, this is a wonderful example of the healing properties of art. I believe the asymmetrical design Carl tagged is more authentic to the graffiti movement than the earlier mirrored sketches.

JESSICA HISCHE I love that the artist gave himself the challenge of doing this a bit asymmetrically instead of just flipping the characters exactly along the center line. I've never done graffiti but could imagine it's a very challenging medium to work with. An excellent first attempt!

JOHN LANGDON The work of most accomplished ambigram artists tends toward either typographic or calligraphic traditions, so it's a real pleasure to see our art form taken to a much less familiar, uh, "canvas." By strictest ambigram standards, the drawings in Figure 2.2 are the most successful. In the spray-painted version, slight liberties have been taken with the most challenging glyph—the E/P—allowing each to read ideally as we face the wall, whereas they would suffer, just a little, if we were to see the piece in the rearview mirror. The E/P would be difficult to pull off in a typographic style; that glyph and the medium are in perfect harmony.

MAGGIE MACNAB I happen to be a fan of graffiti. I know this isn't the case for many. My preference is illustrated social commentary rather than words alone (which are more associated with tagging), but we are talking about ambigrams here. I responded well to the designer picking up on the opportunity to use mirror symmetry in this design. I would have liked to see the first rough explored further in Figure 2.2, because the larger M serves as a fulcrum to balance the teeter-tottering halves. Coming from an art background, I also feel positive about the necessary roughness of the execution (very fitting for the application), as well as the handmade quality of it.

SCOT MORRIS This graffito has two Ts and an M that are already bilaterally symmetrical. I like the freedom Carl takes with making one side of the design not quite a reflection of the other side but close enough to give overall balance.

SCOTT KIM Graffiti art, like jazz, is a cultural treasure. Here, Carl Mehling delivers a passionate tribute to his disabled graffiti artist friend. It's wonderful how the challenge of creating the right ambigram for the right person can lead you to try things you've never tried before.

STEFAN G. BUCHER Oh, I love the E to P maneuver in this one. And the fact that it was done as a friendly challenge makes it even better. I hope somebody puts up a giant mirror next to this wall so minds can be properly blown.

Figure 2.1 The finished poster with the ambigrams and secondary lettering.

Blazing, which I designed in 2010, is my best ambigram to date. It has been released as a limited edition print exclusively through PicturesOnWalls, which sells the work of some extremely talented and well-known artists, including Banksy and Antony Micallef.

Let me give you a little background information about Blazing: Generally speaking, the art that has always moved and impressed me most has been work that brings together the highest levels of beauty, originality, and craftsmanship. So the idea behind Blazing was to try to really push myself beyond what I'd achieved in previous prints in terms of these three qualities.

As with some of my other labour-intensive pieces, I spent a long time thinking about the project before I actually started drawing seriously. Lots of research and planning went into it, and I produced hundreds of sketches and scribbles (*Figures 2.2* and *2.3*). The print is an invertible

ambigram, but I didn't want that to detract aesthetically, as is often the case. The print had to be legible and beautiful in its own right; the fact that it's an ambigram was the icing on the cake.

Figure 2.2 Initial sketch.

Figure 2.3 Detailed sketch.

Figure 2.4 Detailed sketch 2.

I'm not religious, so I use the word Heaven in this piece simply to describe a condition or place of great happiness, delight, or pleasure. The words stem from the idea of dressing beautiful concepts in beautiful letters. Many people say that beauty is subjective, but it's never felt that way to me. Some shapes are inherently beautiful and some aren't. The most beautiful lettering styles to me are often the most cursive, so "The Shimmering..." line adopts a highly cursive, flourished, formal script style (*Figure 2.4*). I've contrasted it with a lettering style that I wanted to look strong, majestic, and timeless—as if it's inscribed in stone or metal and is ancient and cutting edge at the same time.

I hope that the deep passion I feel for letterforms comes across in this piece. Blazing draws from some of the most beautiful lettering styles in history, but, I hope, presents something that appears fundamentally modern, original, and beautiful.

Figure 2.5 Details of the final lettering.

CHERYL SAVALA This design by Seb is by far one of the most brilliant lettering designs of our century. To conceptualize an ambigram from a single word certainly requires expertise and attention. To design a rotational ambigram with two to three words reaches a level of excellence achieved by few. But to create an ambigram of this magnitude in complexity and beauty is simply unsurpassed. I am in awe, Seb.

JESSICA HISCHE I have been a huge admirer of Seb's work for some time now, so it's so fun to see him included here among the ambigrams and to hear a bit about his process! I love how legible but still how beautiful the poster is, and although the words are ambigrams, the phrase takes on slightly different meanings when you read it from bottom to top or top to bottom. Beautiful letterforms, beautiful vector drafting, excellent use of ornament, which adds to rather than distracts from the letters. Love it!

JOHN LANGDON This is such an exquisite and breathtaking piece of lettering art that the ambigrammatic feature is almost incidental. Although I am loath to critique such a wonderful piece of work, there's one glyph—considering the ambigram on its own—that could be slightly better: The H and the N (not one glyph!) could work better as lowercase characters, but that would have diminished the overall design. The right decision was made. Although S/e and s/h are not easy glyphs to create with the seemingly effortless grace that we see here, they simply take their respective places in this heavenly chorus.

SCOT MORRIS A yeoman's job of handling three different inversion ambigrams in one design. It is easy to read, and Seb has nicely kept the letter styles consistent across all three. Just beautiful.

SCOTT KIM An inspiring, virtuosic composition that shows how far ambigrams can be developed visually. Legibility is high here thanks to four words that all work quite naturally as ambigrams. Notice that each large word is a self-contained ambigram, so the order of words reverses when the piece is turned upside down. The composition is so strong that it strikes you first as a beautiful work of art; only later does it dawn on you that it can be turned upside down.

STEFAN G. BUCHER Showoff. There are so many stylish maneuvers going on here that should, by all rights, have failed either individually or piled on top of each other. But dammit, here we are! It's a gorgeous piece that combines so many different modes of lettering and ornamentation that it should just be a hodgepodge, but it just feels sumptuous and delightful! AND it's a successful ambigram. Damn you, Lester!

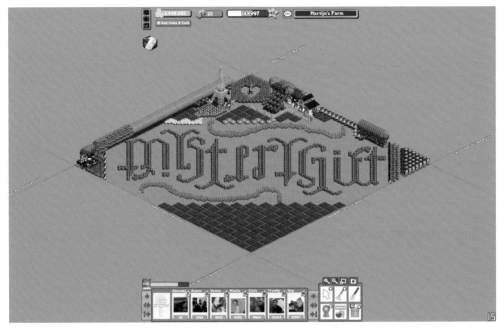

Figure 2.1 The finished ambigram.

The MysteryGift ambigram was inspired
by the game *FarmVille* on Facebook in
the spring of 2010. For those unfamiliar
with the game, here is the gist of it: You
are a farmer with a square of land to plant
and harvest your own digitally delicious
crops on. You can also have farm animals
and decorate your area with farm-related
items, such as hay bales, fences, and trees.
In fact, it was those very hay bales that
actually allowed me to create ambigrams in
FarmVille. While browsing on Facebook, I
found a group of people that made artwork/
images on their farms using all different
kinds of coloured hay bales, and I immediately wanted to see if I could create hay bale
ambigrams!

I started small with a rendition of my Art
ambigram, which looked pretty decent, but
there was plenty of room for improvement.
After deciding to work on a slightly larger
and thicker scale to allow more detail, I created the word Animal, which looked much
better than my first attempt.

Thereafter, I continued with a series of
holiday- and farm-themed ambigrams until
FarmVille temporarily added special Gifts
that one player could send to another. I
collected a bunch of them and placed them
in different locations on my farm just for
decorative purposes. However, it didn't take
long until I started drawing an ambigram of
this so-called Mystery Gift on paper. While
doing so, I asked my fellow farmers for
help in collecting as many Gifts as I could
within the time span they were available.
It took me two weeks or so to accumulate
an amount that would allow me to actually

start "drawing" in the game. This gave me plenty of time to think of ideas.

As the sketches show, the main shape of the ambigram formed rather naturally and didn't need many adaptations or decorations for it to be readable (*Figure 2.2*). However, I did want to see if it would be possible to create an ambigram that read Mystery one way and Gift the other way. That proved to be quite tricky due to the difference in the length of the words. I had to turn seven letters into four! It would not have been the end of the world if three of the letters in the shortest word were not single, linear letters ("ift"). The shape of those three letters combined would easily fit in the letter M alone (as you can see in the MysteryGift ambigram), but then I'd have to design a letter G that turned into YSTERY when turned upside down, which to me seemed fairly impossible.

To solve this problem, I had to grab every possibility of turning one letter of the word Gift into at least two letters of the word Mystery to restore the balance. That's when I decided to move the letter T one "leg" backwards inside the M so that most of that letter was used for the T and the rest would be half of the F. Notice that I split apart the F and G to allow for more letters to make use of their shapes.

In the end, I tore up the G so drastically that I could then turn that single letter into the four letters TERY. This produced a great result, although readability suffered quite a bit, and I realized this complex ambigram would never be compatible with the blocky Gifts in *FarmVille*. Hence, the

Figure 2.2 Initial sketches.

Mystery/Gift ambigram had to be put on hold for this particular project.

Continuing with my initial approach but in a less curly style, I again kept the little Gifts in mind. It was a real challenge to work with these special limitations: There was no way of "cheating" by using decorations to make letters, nor the ability to make letters go through one another, because squared Gifts and high detail do not mix well.

By the time I had the ambigram straightened out on paper (*Figure 2.3*), I had collected a hoard of Gifts and started to make room on my farm. I cleared a canvas and calculated the exact middle to ensure that it would fit or at least be evenly distributed. Even after collecting hundreds of Gifts, I still couldn't build more than YSTERYG and had to depend on help from my friends for a while longer.

Eventually, we did make it just in time before the Gifts expired and became unavailable. Thanks to my helpful farmer associates I collected the 704 Mystery Gifts required to finish the ambigram (*Figure 2.1*)! And it felt more special than the other ambigrams I made, even those I created in *FarmVille*, because I depended solely on the help from other people, which made it a collaborative effort rather than an individual project (Figure 2.4). It's this one-of-a-kind teamwork combined with the temporary nature of the Gifts that turned this ambigram into something truly unique.

Figure 2.3 Detailed sketch.

Figure 2.4 Ambigram development in progress within the Farmville game environment.

CHERYL SAVALA The interactive and community components of how this all came together is very inspiring. What a fantastic way to spread the art form to other media. In terms of legibility, there are some challenges with the reduced and simplified form, but considering the context, Martijn has created quite a distinct piece of work.

JESSICA HISCHE I love how collaborative the process of making this ambigram was, and what an inventive medium to work with! I would be delighted to randomly stumble upon this little piece of ambigram art within the game. I couldn't imagine racing against the clock to gather enough gifts to make this possible. The end result is super fun, and I love how some of the letter combinations worked out. My favorite is the YS/G flip.

JOHN LANGDON Ambigrams are for people who like challenges, and as if creating one weren't challenging enough on its own, making one to fit into the gridded constraints of a *FarmVille* image is an impressive feat. The payback to the artist is that we have been somewhat conditioned to forgive minor oddities that crop up here by way of traditional sampler lettering. It's clear from the sketches that MYSTERYGIFT would succeed as a fully drawn and rendered ambigram. The most impressive lettering achievement here is the G made from the combination of the Y and S.

SCOT MORRIS A distribution of hay bales in *FarmVille*: surely a unique medium! Martijn refers to his ambigrams of Art and Animal: I would like to have seen these. The capital G on Gift makes the break between the two words clear.

SCOTT KIM A nicely readable ambigram rendered within the coarse grid of an online game. Note that the only uppercase letter is the G, which starts the second word—good for legibility. Players in games like *FarmVille* often create elaborate murals like this, a testament to the universal need for self-expression.

STEFAN G. BUCHER Hey! Are you browsing through this book without reading the text? Read this case study! It's excellent!

NIKITA PROKHOROV A very unusual medium, and Martijn makes the most of it! Although the initial development is done on paper, this case study is a testament to the versatility of the ambigram. Remember that paper/pencil/pen or the computer and software aren't the only mediums out there!

Figure 2.1 The final ambigram in two different styles.

They say that children can be inspirational, and in my case this turned out to be very true indeed! My wife Fa and I were reading a bedtime story to our daughters about the different birds in a jungle, and the word kingfisher appeared several times in the book. Call it subconscious wanderings if you may, but I was pulled in by how the letters in the word were cooperative enough to be formed into an ambigram.

After the little ones went to their own jungle dreams, and Fa rested with her book, I went to the desk and armed myself with several sheets of paper and a pencil. I started by writing the word kingfisher in different styles (*Figure 2.2*) and confirming that the letters were indeed cooperative for an ambigram makeover. And they were!

The next step was to develop the letter combinations (*Figure 2.3*). For some letter combinations, there already is a ready-made "formula," whereas others need tweaking and additional exploration. In my first attempt I saw the k–er, in–sh, and g–fi flips. The k–er and g–fi looked interesting, but the s seemed too difficult to read.

My second attempt was more straightforward: a one-to-one letter flip. The central ngfish worked very well because these letters offered similar strokes and shapes with their corresponding letters, so I decided to stick to this formula. The ki–er, on the other hand, looked out of place, especially the awkward uppercase ER at the end of the word, which needed some amendments.

For the third formula, I improvised to address the ki–er. I noticed that the k had the extra strokes that I could merge with the i to form an e. Here, I drew inspiration from an earlier piece, a John Mayer ambigram, which was presented in a successful stencil-like font. This font enabled the

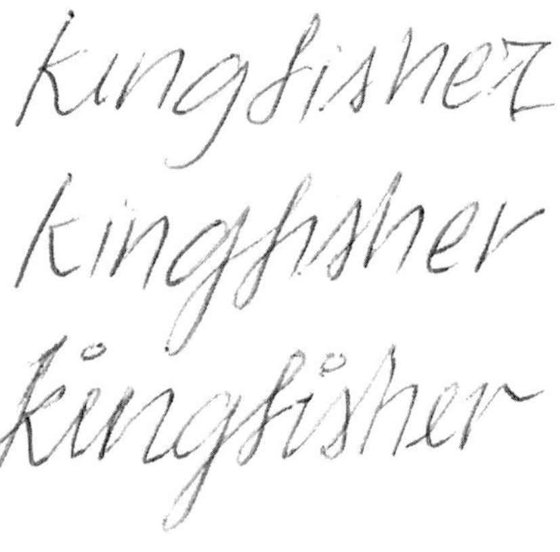

Figure 2.2 Initial sketches.

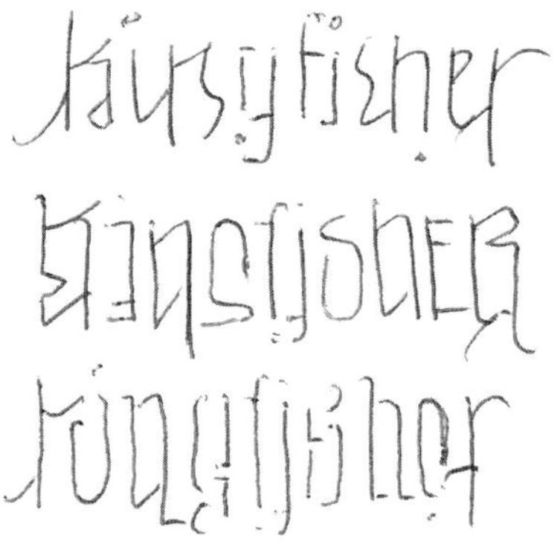

Figure 2.3 Various letter flip exploration.

Figure 2.4 Detailed letterform exploration.

smooth transitions of reading one letter to the next, even with disjointed strokes. Hence, the ki–er formula was formed.

The detail for the k–r solution (*Figure 2.4*) I later found to be awkward due to the final r being in uppercase. Moving on, I created the sketch in *Figure 2.5*. But there were still some problems. Aesthetically, a stencil form did not sit well with some gothic influence. It made the piece look messy and unfocused.

The next solution (*Figure 2.6*) produced a simplified rendering of the previous version with cleaner strokes and simpler lines. I was pleased at how the ki–er still worked well here with just a slight hint of the e. Another pleasing outcome was the g–s solution. The height of the strokes helped with the differentiation of the two letters in their respective orientation.

The last version (*Figure 2.7*) further standardized the letters: I removed the connecting lines to make it more stencil-like. The letters were arranged with the appropriate spacing, and the r was tweaked ever so slightly to provide for a more consistent overall look. The final solutions for the ambigram of the word kingfisher were clean, modern, and legible.

The process for this ambigram design is definitely one I'll continue to use. Although choosing a suitable word is an easy enough process (with practice and observation, of course!), sometimes designers tend to be content with the normal letter-to-letter formula. When I wrote that first k–r formula—subconsciously, like it came so naturally, if I may add—I didn't realize how awkward the word would look in a mixture of uppercase and lowercase letters. This forced me to find an alternative, which made it turn out better than I expected! What I like about the final

Figure 2.5 Detailed stylistic exploration.

Figure 2.6 Detailed style exploration 1.

Figure 2.7 Detailed style exploration 2.

solution is that it doesn't look like a "traditional" ambigram—those that are steeped in (pseudo)gothic fonts or rely heavily on the cursive forms.

The final ambigram (*Figure 2.1*) was decidedly left as it is for two reasons. First, due to time constraints as teachers and as parents, designers today are more inclined to do freehand ambigram sketches. Second, even without spending hours in front of various drawing programs (which are often not needed, as shown here), the solution is still readable and stands on its own as a successful ambigram. These two factors only strengthened the fact that anyone with decent skills in observation and scribbling can attempt this art.

Inspiration comes from everywhere, really, if you're ready to be inspired. Always keep a pencil and paper on you. And always be willing to look at things from different angles. Wait; that's "ambigramism" for you!

CHERYL SAVALA What is so interesting to me about this case study is the two completely different stylistic interpretations NAGFA developed. The more traditional blackletter design seemed nearly effortless from this talented designer. But the block-formed lettering design is more legible, distinct, and memorable.

JESSICA HISCHE This ambigram is quite readable, particularly in the more traditional blackletter form. I'd be interested in seeing what the stencil version looks like filled in too! The G/S flip is my favorite in both, but I also love how the K/ER is handled in the more stenciled option. The E is a little tough to read, but I think in context it works.

JOHN LANGDON I wish that one of the final two versions of KINGFISHER had been refined to a point of finished art. Either one would likely be a beauty, and it's disappointing to see them both fall short. The blackletter version has some very pleasing letterforms, most notably the K/R and the g/s. I find the f particularly disturbing, because the too large dot on the I severely injures its upper structure, whereas a more gracefully completed f could have dotted the I effortlessly. It would be fun to see the fully refined stencil version, especially the ki/er. The g might be a bit too fragmented, though, to be fully successful.

SCOT MORRIS I like step 1 when NAGFA confirms that the letters of the word kingfisher "are indeed cooperative for an ambigram makeover." I liked the lengthy consideration of the work behind making KI into ER. As an aside, when I first looked at Figure 2.6, I thought it read "Janet"!

SCOTT KIM Two quite successful ambigrams in two utterly different lettering styles. Notice how the two ambigrams use completely different solutions to KI/ER. I encourage all ambigram designers to look for the second solution; sometimes you will find something even better.

STEFAN G. BUCHER I like that NAGFA left these ambigrams loose and light. It's hard to say for sure without a direct comparison to a clean digital version, but I suspect that keeping the designs in sketch form makes them easier to parse. My eye is in a different mode looking at sketched lettering than it is looking at highly rendered pieces.

Figure 2.1 The final solution for John Langdon.

Figure 2.2 The final solution for Scott Kim.

Two individuals have inspired most, if not all, newcomers to the art form of symmetrical writing, or ambigrams: John Langdon and Scott Kim. John Langdon is a typographer, artist, illustrator, and author. Scott Kim is an artist, author, puzzle designer, and computer game designer.

For many years after seeing the famous *Angels & Demons* ambigram by John Langdon for Dan Brown's best-selling novel, I was fascinated with ambigrams and studied the portfolios of Langdon and Kim. I played with nothing but rotational designs, which was very satisfying and a lot of fun, but after a while, I had experimented with so many different letter combinations that some of the mystery and challenge was gone. I then started experimenting with a different type of ambigram called a *reflective*, or *mirror*, ambigram. To me, these mirrors were very different and extremely challenging, and they quickly became my preferred type of ambigram. They forced me to develop a completely different set of techniques and tools. For this reason, I've selected a mirror ambigram for this case study. And why not take on the two ambigram pioneers, John Langdon and Scott Kim?

I'm always a little apprehensive creating ambigrams for other ambigram artists because I'm sure the artists have already explored every conceivable possibility with their own name. But why not?

JOHN LANGDON AMBIGRAM

My first attempt at the John Langdon design mainly followed a letter-for-letter approach (*Figure 2.3*). This is usually how I start the exploration process: J = (N reflected), O = (O reflected), H = (D reflected), N = (G reflected), and L+A = (N reflected).

For the most part, I was pleased with the outcome of this design but was a little bothered with the central portion of the design. To me, the spacing between the L-A-N did not match the spacing between the other letters, so I continued to explore different possibilities.

For my second attempt (*Figure 2.4*), I tried to force a natural center. The A was an obvious choice. Once I placed the A, I sketched from the inside out. Instead of looking at each letter as a whole, I tried to visualize each letter as a combination of multiple parts. With the exception of the ends of the design (JO-ON), I explored creating letterforms that were made up of pieces from letterforms of the reflected side of the design. To make this work, it required a "lateral shift" in one of the letters, so I decided to hide the arched portion of the D as the flares of the H on the reflected side. I purposefully made a break at the bottom portion of the arc to make it easier to accept the H. Also, I slightly separated the base of the G to split the H and N in JOHN.

At that point, I felt as though I could make this a more successful design due to the spacing between all of the letterforms, so I worked to refine the design.

Figure 2.3 Initial sketch for John Langdon.

Figure 2.4 Second option for the John Langdon ambigram.

SCOTT KIM AMBIGRAM

Right off the bat I saw Scott Kim's name as a huge challenge. None of the letterforms seemed to work well together, and there was no obvious center. The M was an important first hurdle to clear, so I started there (*Figure 2.5*). Typically, I'll write the word or name forward and backward in as many possible styles as I can think of—cursive, caps, lowercase, mixed, and so on. This was my first idea and quick sketch. For me, the K and S were the most difficult letterforms to deal with, so I explored using a portion of the K to double as the base of the S (*Figure 2.6*) on the reflected side. I liked the concept a lot and thought it had great potential, so I decided to use this initial sketch as the basis for the final design.

The final versions (*Figures 2.1* and *2.2*) I drew using a ballpoint pen. Although the computer allows for very precise and aesthetically sound designs, there is something personal and unique about a hand-drawn ambigram. And because John and Scott's work inspired me on a very personal level, I wanted to make sure that the ambigrams "reflected" that.

Figure 2.5 Initial sketch for Scott Kim.

Figure 2.6 Secondary sketch for Scott Kim.

CHERYL SAVALA Clayton's personal design aesthetics come through these two designs loud and clear—elegant, curvelinear, fluid integration, and sharpened technique. These two designs are certainly a strong reflection of Clayton's admiration and mastery of lessons learned.

JESSICA HISCHE What a wonderful homage to two talented artists! Both of these ambigrams are very legible, and I love the liberties taken with the big swashes in the Scott Kim ambigram. The drawing could be cleaned up ever so slightly (some of the curves could be smoothed out a touch), but I do appreciate wanting to do these by hand because of the personal nature of the subject. The Scott Kim ambigram almost feels like a crown, which I love, considering it was done out of respect for him as an artist.

JOHN LANGDON Rotational ambigrams benefit from the fact that we tend to read the tops of letters more than the bottoms. Mirror-image ambigrams don't get to that benefit, so I am awed by the degree of success achieved by these two examples. The OHN/GDO is incredible. The monoweight character of the A and L diminish their beauty by comparison to the other letters. The n is probably a pretty challenging read. SCOTTKIM, although simply gorgeous, would likely prove difficult for the average reader. The K and M are the most recognizable letters, and the three central verticals become somewhat of a separate, standalone entity.

SCOTT KIM Clayton Mabey takes on mirror symmetry, which he, like I, find more difficult than rotational symmetry. His search for solutions led to a quirky, spiky, Tim Burtonesque style for JOHN LANGDON and an equally quirky, handlebar moustache/overstuffed armchair style for my name.

SCOT MORRIS Clayton had to work with the two iconic names as given. He niccly shows how the construction of a bilaterally symmetrical design differs from the more common rotation ambigram. I find both names quite legible, but part of that is because I already know the names. My guest judge was able to make out John Langdon but had difficulty reading the Scott Kim ambigram. Scott's first name is much more legible than his last name.

STEFAN G. BUCHER This takes us back to the problem with "syzygy." If you wouldn't recognize the word in its regular form, you certainly won't make it out as an ambigram. With these two beautiful ambigrams, context is king. Seen in isolation, it takes a while to sort out that you're looking at names, which becomes the key. On a business card or letterhead they will work immediately. Not realizing that I was looking for a name, I initially read Scott Kim as "gnomon" or "Nottkon." Going from an o to an i in a flowing script is a tough challenge.

Figure 2.1 The final ambigram.

Every ambigram I create begins the same way, which is to determine my subject matter. For this "unseen" ambigram, a good friend of mine asked if I would (or could) create something for his hip-hop dance company. I agreed, as I usually do, to take on the task of creating said ambigram. And create I did.

My first step is always to write the word/name/phrase in many different ways. Usually, I write the word right-side up and then upside down in both uppercase and lowercase letters (*Figure 2.2*). Sometimes I'll use cursive; sometimes I'll use different variations of letters. In this particular case, I stuck with lowercase letters.

Next, I begin to look for similarities in the way the letters line up. For example, in my initial sketches I saw a natural ambigram where the u/n matched up and also where the s matched up with itself. All I really

had to do then was make the two e's look like an upside-down n. As you can see in *Figures 2.2a*, *2.2b*, and *2.2c*, I played around with how to make the ends of the n morph into e's.

After I figure out the initial "solve" and how to make the letters work together (so an upside-down letter looks like its right-side-up counterpart), I begin to create a theme in my mind of how I want my ambigram's font to look. My target audience is always on my mind when I try to come up with something personal to fit it. Therefore, I thought about how the unseen ambigram could be stylized to fit my friend's dance company.

Initially, for this design, I conjured up a much simpler design (*Figure 2.3a*) than the final model. After looking it over and trying to create it in a "thicker" font (*Figure 2.3b*), I gave up. Soon thereafter, I

Figure 2.2 Initial sketches.

redirected my energy and decided that this design needed a "graffiti" sort of feel. I had just had the pleasure of catching a performance of a stunning dance troupe, and all of the hand-crafted graffiti used in the performance stuck out most in my memory. So my quest to emulate that font began.

After attempting to create a graffiti font for the ambigram, I unfortunately was not able to generate anything I liked (*Figures 2.4a* and *2.4b*). It was then that I decided to research graffiti art from all over the globe, ranging from the United States to Europe and Asia. I paid attention to the different font styles, colors, and characters that went into every piece of art. Then, after a random epiphany, I shifted several letters, getting rid of my natural s ambigram, which

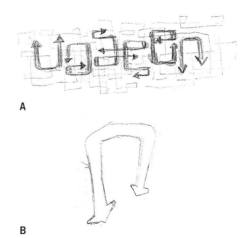

Figure 2.3 Initial style exploration.

ended up being a great decision! I was able to maintain continuity with all of the letters being lowercase, create a "graffiti-style" font to go with the theme I was hoping for, and construct all the letter combinations (*Figures 2.5a, 2.5b,* and *2.5c*).

My next step was and is the most time-consuming part, and is sometimes the most difficult. To make everything symmetrical, I used a makeshift carbon transfer by coloring the entire backside of the drawing with pencil and then transferring it to my final paper choice. Once all the letters were grouped, I went through the same process to make my ambigram half into a whole.

When the design was finished, I used the carbon-transfer method again to transfer the ambigram onto the paper used for the final design. I prefer Bristol and typically use a variety of ink pens of different line thicknesses to add a bit of depth to each ambigram. In this step, you must use extreme caution, because if you make a mistake, there's no turning back. You can't erase the ink, and the process of getting the ambigram to the final stage is time-consuming and tedious: To make a mistake could mean having to start over completely! Lucky for me, the end result of my unseen ambigram turned out great (*Figure 2.1*)!

Figure 2.4 Secondary style exploration.

Figure 2.5 Detailed stylistic exploration.

CHERYL SAVALA The challenge for me in this design is the mixture of organic shapes and rigid angular outlining. The detail in the letterforms is very unique, yet the line work and inferred dimensionality diminish the legibility, ironically making the word truly "unseen." By incorporating color, value, and even perhaps a little rendering, this design may reveal itself more easily to the untrained eye—and the target audience.

JESSICA HISCHE Before reading any of the artist's own words, I look straight at the end result to see just how legible the ambigrams are without any real context. This one is super legible, and the letterforms are really very inventive. It's a really fun mark for a hip-hop dance company, and I could imagine enjoying reading it right-side up and upside down as dancers tossed their bodies this way and that.

JOHN LANGDON One seldom sees a graffiti piece of this style and complexity without color and tonal variation, and I suspect that with those attributes this piece could go from being technically successful to being a knockout. Although it's not hugely challenging, the various letter combinations are handled very well, and the creased and crinkled effects, the letters, the heavy outline, and the arrows are all authentic attributes of a wall work.

SCOTT KIM Usually, ambigrams are not legible enough to function as logos. After all, the first function of any logo is to be read. Fortunately, UNSEEN works easily as an ambigram, so Jen Winklepleck was able to focus her energy on expressing the spirit of this hip-hop group through the style of the lettering. As her sketches show, her hard work paid off.

STEFAN G. BUCHER As with TEMPT and Kingfisher, this ambigram shows that a looser style gets you past many obstacles. Graffiti lettering is already so highly stylized that even regular tags require more decoding than reading. None of these letterforms feel out of place. In fact, they're such a good fit for the genre that one might miss that this is an ambigram. Unseen, indeed. Adding the flipped character is a great hint.

Figure 2.1 The final ambigram.

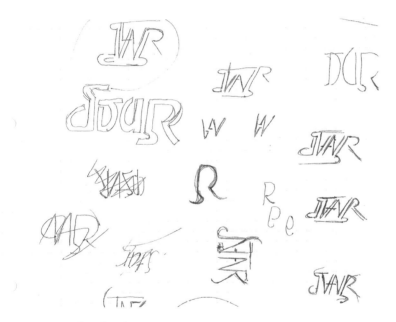

Figure 2.2 Initial exploration.

The Snapstar ambigram started out as a commission piece: Two students who planned to start a company named Snapstar to produce and sell snapback caps asked me if I would design an ambigram brand logo for them. Even though they would not be able to pay me sufficiently, the thought of having one of my ambigrams printed or stitched on a collection of clothes (hey, why stop with the caps?) was pretty daunting, but I agreed. With no further information than the company's name at my disposal, I started looking for a way to create a Snapstar ambigram.

The search for a solution, the puzzling, and the mixture of mental exercise and design are my favorite parts of ambigram creation. A few thoughts immediately run through my mind: Is it even possible to create an ambigram from that word? If so, can I design it in an aesthetically pleasing and legible way? I'm pretty obsessed with consistent-looking letters, so will it be possible to achieve that look? Will I have to (hopefully not) mix uppercase and lower-case letters?

Figure 2.3 SN/AR glyph exploration.

My first scribbles are usually pretty rough. I begin by writing down the word in uppercase and lowercase letters, starting from both the beginning and the end of the word, and then take a look at the cards I've been dealt. These doodles are hardly legible to anyone but me, but usually they are sufficient to decide if an ambigram is feasible or not (*Figure 2.2*).

While scribbling the Snapstar sketches, I realized that the word could not be turned into an ambigram as naturally as I initially thought; there would be some obstacles to overcome. Even though the major part of Snapstar would be pretty easy to flip, the SN/AR glyph proved to be tricky. If I wanted to keep the nicely flowing A/A flip, the N was interfering with the S/R combination. Therefore, I had to find a way to merge the N with the S, which I did, or so I thought (*Figure 2.3*).

Figure 2.4 Initial style exploration.

Figure 2.6 Exploration of a style with fewer details.

Figure 2.7 Additional sketch exploration.

Figure 2.5 Initial stylistic explorations.

Figure 2.8 The final overall style selected by the clients.

Because I was pleased with my solution, I started to scribble the ambigram in various styles (*Figure 2.4*). And because it would be a brand logo, I opted for a more stylized look. I created some quick versions of my drafts in Adobe Illustrator and sent it to my customers to see which direction they would prefer (*Figure 2.5*). The customers chose the hand-written style and told me that the logo would be stitched on the side of the caps. That meant that I had to use thicker lines and fewer details because of the stitching process (*Figure 2.6*). The clients liked the overall look of the design but informed me that it had two flaws: 1) they didn't like the center portion of the ambigram and 2) it wasn't legible enough. Once again, it looked like I had been suffering

from a severe case of routine blindness! I was so sure of the legibility of my design that I forgot to test it on "regular" people, which was a bad mistake, especially for a design that would be a logo.

After some belated testing, the problem became clear: The Sn/R flip was too difficult to read and wasn't functional. I reverted to paper once more and found the right solution (*Figure 2.7*). Luckily, the customers wanted a hand-written style; otherwise, the solution would have been very tough to implement (*Figure 2.8*).

At last, everybody was able to read the ambigram without any problems, and the customers were happy with the style. I put some finishing touches on the design, and the final result was a success (*Figure 2.1*).

JUDGE'S COMMENTS

CHERYL SAVALA What makes Bastian's final design work more successfully than the previous is that he shifted the lettering off the baseline. It becomes more legible as two words and better personifies common characteristics of typical action-sports logotypes. Sometimes it takes a few misses to get to this point, but Bastian surely had patience and persistence to keep going.

JESSICA HISCHE I loved seeing the process of this one come together and the huge variety of styles that the artist was working with! I was surprised at how legible all of the explorations were, not just the final result. It's obvious the artist had a lot of fun working on this one, and it shows in the end result. I really like the mono-weight option shown in Figure 2.4, too.

JOHN LANGDON SNAPSTAR is quite a good ambigram. The SN/AR is very smartly conceived and perfectly executed. And, although weaker than the other letters, the S in STAR is surprisingly successful in part due to a very forgiving casual style and the intelligent placement tucked in under the P—where the strong TAR handles the responsibility of communicating a familiar word. For comparison, in Figure 2.6 it comes dangerously close to reading SNAESTAR. If this ambigram is used well, it could be a very successful logo.

MAGGIE MACNAB It's always a challenge to use an ambigram as a logo because of the inherent complexity of this design form. This issue is directly linked to length: The more characters involved in the ambigram, the more detail there is to resolve. One of the good things about this particular name is that each word stands alone. Even so, eight characters is starting to push the limit. I liked some of the initial tightened concepts in Figure 2.5 (particularly the second version with the stylistic borders and integrated star graphic that help to illustrate the name), but agree legibility is a problem. I actually preferred the initial resolution in Figure 2.6 over the final rounded design because I felt it better demonstrated the designer's skill. But design is for the audience first, and the client is the segue to them: The audience ultimately makes the call. This is the difference between art and design.

SCOT MORRIS I like that Bastian tested his design on "regular people" and took their input to refine his rendering. The improved Sn/R flip makes the final version quite legible. I also liked the fact that of all the alternatives shown in Figures 2.5–2.8, the simplest won out. Bastian's original idea was correct: This ambigram would look better on the back of the cap.

SCOTT KIM The difficult S/R combination here is similar to the S/K challenge in the SHARK ATTACK ambigram. Somehow the repeated forms of the letters and consistent uppercase forms make for a logo that is more legible than I would have expected. It's wonderful to see the range of styles explored in Figure 2.5.

STEFAN G. BUCHER Boy, I hope that the people at Snapstar are going to put out the earlier versions of the ambigram as t-shirts. They're all quite cool! I'd buy the blacklister one myself. But in this case legibility has to come first, and it's hard to argue with the chosen solution.

Figure 2.1 The final ambigrams.

To make ambigrams more accessible so people could discover the symmetry of them in an organic way, I tried to think of objects that people naturally turn upside down. Playing cards were the perfect platform.

The first sketches of King of Diamonds were a real struggle (*Figures 2.2* and *2.3*). Because the word Diamonds has more letters than the other suits, my first draft was illegible and forced (*Figure 2.4*). So, I made it The King of Diamonds instead.

To hide the leg of the K in King, the o in Diamonds needed a flourish, which meant a calligraphic style for the ambigram. Another challenge was the a/g. Although an a is difficult to design as an inverted g, the descender of the g was symmetrical on its own; therefore, at the center of the ambigram I wouldn't need to work it into the a (*Figure 2.5*).

The letters in The Queen of Diamonds ambigram also needed to be shuffled around

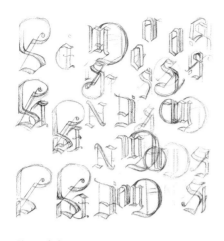

Figure 2.2

Figure 2.3

Figure 2.4

Figure 2.5

Figure 2.6

Figure 2.7

because Queen has more letters. I had two options: use The Queen/Diamonds with "of" in the center or use Queen of/Diamonds. The first option meant I couldn't use the of/Di combination from the The King of Diamonds, but it gave me a neat solution for hiding the descender of the q as part of the f in "of" (*Figure 2.6*).

The Jack of Diamonds ambigram was simpler. The ac/mo was similar to the qu/mo in The Queen of Diamonds. If I could disguise the stem of the k as a flourish, the a/k would work. Similarly, I had to disguise the descender of the j. I referenced old English lettering because of the commonly used flourishes in that style, and it suited the playing card theme.

The Ace of Diamonds fell into place easily. I used the same ac/mo combination from The Jack of Diamonds and the e/a from The Queen of Diamonds.

I wanted each suit to have a different style, so I applied a serif look to the King of Clubs. The u/n naturally worked together, so I started there. The bowl of the g worked with the c, meaning the l would become the descender of the g. I tried hiding the loop of the descender as a flourish in the l (*Figure 2.7*), but that wasn't ideal. Finding a place for the "of" was another issue. Making the descender of the g become the o in "of" solved both problems. The readability of the s suffers because it is so straight, but it was a necessary compromise to keep the style consistent.

For the Ace of Hearts, the e o/ea was simple. The f was close to being an H except for one of the H's stems, which I couldn't incorporate anywhere. But by

Figure 2.8 Detailed sketch exploration.

putting the stem in the center, it didn't need to be part of the f. The c/r caused issues with the spacing of the letterforms. If the c was too close to the A, the r would be less visible. Likewise, if the r was too close to the a, the c would be less visible. It was a case of compromise and finding a balance. I tried A/s but found that A/ts worked better (*Figure 2.8*). People more easily identify letters from the top half of the letterform than the bottom, meaning the curve of the s could easily be disguised as a flourish and not hurt the reading of the A.

JUDGE'S COMMENTS

CHERYL SAVALA A hand well played, Eugene! What an ambitious feat you have in the works with this project. Imagine an entire 52-card deck created in this manner: What an incredible body of work that would be! The biggest obstacle would be creating consistency in letterform stylization, or perhaps each suit is its own unique style? Sounds like an ambigram challenge in the making.

JESSICA HISCHE This is a really great personal assignment! I don't know a designer alive who hasn't dreamt of making a crazy beautiful set of playing cards. They do seem like the perfect opportunity to try out some tricky ambigrams. The artist mentioned wanting to give the different suits different styles, but overall these still feel quite similar to one another. I would say that if he were to consider making these into a real product (please do!) that the style should either be pushed more dramatically in different directions or that it should all just be done in the same style. I could see the "hearts" suit being less blackletter and more script-like, diamonds being more like a faceted blackletter, and so on. Overall, a very cool idea and good execution.

JOHN LANGDON I wish the effort to create all these different ambigrams had been focused on one of them. All of these are almost good ambigrams, and all of them fall short. ACE OF HEARTS is the most successful in terms of readability and character integrity, but it's the least pleasing in style (except for KING OF CLUBS, which is not successful in readability, character integrity, or aesthetics). I love the 1920s storybook style of the other ambigrams, and in some places it works really well. I get the feeling, though, that it was faithfulness to a predetermined style that was the downfall of this group.

SCOT MORRIS These designs are of medium legibility, but this can be excused in light of the difficulty in finding different ways to render so many different words and keep a consistent letter style throughout. The fact that playing cards invert in use makes these designs an especially nice fit. Of the six cards presented, the easiest to read are The Queen of Diamonds and Ace of Hearts. King of Clubs at first glance looks like King of Suns.

SCOTT KIM Like CLEAN/DIRTY, this case study starts by thinking of something that is naturally turned upside down—in this case playing cards. Here it is interesting to note how the same word, in this case DIAMONDS, can turn into several different phrases.

STEFAN G. BUCHER I'm not saying anything about these ambigrams until there is a complete and fully designed deck of ambigram playing cards—at which point I'll start the First Church of Uymatiao.

Figure 2.1 The final ambigram (full alphabet).

Creating an alphabet ambigram is an idea I had been toying with for a long time. For months it lived as doodles in the corners of my school textbooks until it was offered the chance of being published in a textbook where it would actually be appreciated.

Several of my friends used to believe that the technical difficulties in designing an ambigram were nothing more than to use a special font. It is for this reason that I thought up the alphabet ambigram. I could show it to certain members of my naive audience and describe it as a kind of "ambigram font."

Because the alphabet was such a long ambigram, I first split it into numerous sections so I could develop each one as an individual work. Articles written by many ambigram designers say they start the process by choosing an appropriate midpoint for the design, and then work outward. I don't like to use this method because it often results in one side running out of letters before the other. Instead, I start with the beginning of the word and work toward the middle until I begin repeating lines. Using this method, I chose to solve the ABC/XYZ, DE/W, F/V, G/U, H/ST, IJK/QR, L/P, and MNO combinations (*Figure 2.2*).

Originally, the A revolved to be the Z, the B to the Y, and the C to the X (*Figure 2.3*). However, the problem I encountered was that it was almost impossible to make the C/X look tidy. Letters like X (and O for that matter) are always a problem because they are so awkwardly symmetrical! Eventually, after simply drawing the design numerous times and letting evolution take its course, I stumbled upon a new solution. I changed my approach; the X became made up of the C and half of the B, and the ABC linked together to revolve into XYZ. Although this made the A and B more

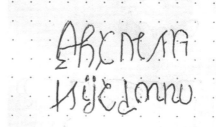

Figure 2.2 Initial sketch.

Figure 2.3 Detailed letter sketch.

awkward, it was still far better than the previous X, so I kept it. Ambigrams are more legible when they use completely different letter groupings in different orientations, so an "insignificant" gap between two letters becomes a main part of the rotated letter, as in the MNO solution.

The solution I am most proud is of the IJK/QR combination. Under close scrutiny its legibility is not very clear, but when read in the context of the other letters, the J and the stem of the K somehow separate into their individual counterparts. When designing ambigrams, it is important to identify the features of a letter that make it recognisable. In the same way that a good caricature artist can draw a geometrically incorrect portrait of a face while still retaining the likeness, a good ambigram artist (or an ambigrammatist) should understand all the ways it is possible to distort a character while maintaining its legibility. This is the reason the K is still readable without a proper stem.

Another problem with designing such long ambigrams is that although it is nice to keep the writing style consistent throughout, sometimes the manipulations needed to maintain legibility violate the "rules" of the chosen writing style. For this reason, the M looks somewhat Celtic, whereas the T is very Roman; the H is curvy, whereas the R is stiff. The even positioning of letters, the identical serifs, and the stylistic colours and outlines help to keep all the characters proportionate and matching. Fortunately, this design had no repeating letters, so I didn't have to make identical characters look identical.

The final solution was drawn in a Humanist-looking script (*Figure 2.4*). I then scanned it into my computer and traced

over the lines using Adobe Illustrator. Because I wanted to keep all of the characters proportionate, I copied and pasted all the stems, serifs, and the bowls on the B, P, and R. Tracing the lines also allowed me to make adjustments, which would have probably involved lengthier revisions if done by hand. I experimented with several different looks but in the end decided that I wanted it to look elegant, squeaky clean, and velvety smooth. Next, I warped it using a fisheye warp and then applied a few outlines and Adobe Photoshop effects. After adding a stylish border, the desired effect was complete (*Figure 2.1*). Flourishes—as they should generally be—were used relatively rarely and only to hide an important stroke in the inverted text. You can see this in the curl running off the F and the loop coming from the arm of the K.

This is definitely my most ambitious design yet, and I hope that in some way it has contributed to the world of ambigrams.

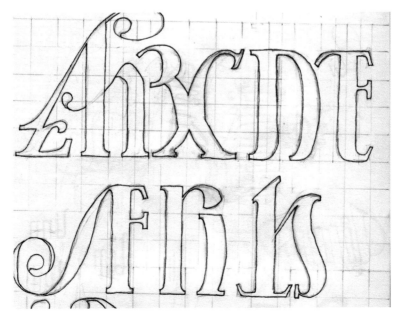

Figure 2.4 Detailed letter sketch (full alphabet).

JUDGE'S COMMENTS

CHERYL SAVALA A truly ambitious work worthy of a beautifully letterpress poster design. It is unclear what the purpose or need is for the fisheye distortion at the end of the process. It looks stunning with or without.

JESSICA HISCHE I love the idea that something so customized could be seen as a "font" to a naive onlooker. I couldn't imagine how challenging this was to create and how many different iterations the artist must have gone through before reaching the final result. There are areas that are more legible than others. I love the HIKJ/QRST flip: It's really, really awesome. The BC/X is definitely a stretch, as is the W (the DE is perfectly readable, but I think the W just works because of context). The style is really interesting, and I like that the decorative swashes are kept to a minimum and are a lot lighter in weight than the rest of the alphabet. I'm sure plenty of people would love to have this piece of artwork on their walls!

JOHN LANGDON The highest praise I could offer with regard to this alphabet ambigram challenge is for the courage it took to take it on. Ultimately, I'm afraid, it was a bit too big a bite. The one flash of brilliance here is the IJ ligature, which creates the R. The G/U glyph is very nice as well, and the ST/H and M/NO deserve mention too. The style was well chosen and plays a significant part in those successes. But the Y creates a strong H between the A and the B; the E was not crafted in a way that would help create the W; the V necessitates an incongruous flourish on the F. Overall, this admirable attempt has too many awkward parts.

SCOT MORRIS Out of the 15 case studies this is probably the most difficult ambigram to render, because it is so long. It is intriguing to consider Kai's unusual attack on the problems by starting at the outside and working in as opposed to the usual tack of starting at the middle and working out. I was especially interested in his description of the difficulties encountered in maintaining a consistent writing style while maintaining legibility—the necessary violation of the "rules" of a chosen font. I guess I don't have much to say except Bravo! This wins my vote as the best of all the case studies.

SCOTT KIM An interesting take on a worthy and difficult challenge. I tried and failed at this ambigram many years ago, and decided to do a mirror-symmetric alphabet instead. Although I like the overall graphic effect of this ambigram, I find many of the letters too distorted for my taste, which makes me want to try again to see if I can do better. How would you draw a rotationally symmetric alphabet?

STEFAN G. BUCHER Although I realize that the term "showoff" applies to ambigrammists by definition, this takes showing off to new heights. Kai Hammond clearly designed this ambigram alphabet in an attempt to make everybody else feel bad about their own skills. He has succeeded. I'm going to say that the F is a dirty trick and that the G and the L need some work, but I do so purely to keep a little dignity as I slink away to my desk.

AMBIGRAM LEGEND

This chapter showcases nearly 200 ambigrams from around the world. Some of these ambigrams can be classified into one category, whereas others will encompass more than one category. The following legend will help you classify the ambigrams on the subsequent pages. To fully discover some of the ambigrams, you may have to turn the book or hold it up to a mirror!

Rotational ambigram. These ambigrams are rotated either 90 degrees or 180 degrees to reveal the same word as the original.

Symbiotogram. These ambigrams are rotated either 90 degrees or 180 degrees to reveal a word different from the original.

Reflection. These ambigrams are reflected/mirrored vertically, horizontally, or at 45 degrees.

Chain ambigram. The word(s) in these ambigrams form a repeating linear or circular chain.

Figure/ground ambigram. An ambigram where the negative space between the letters forms another word.

Multilingual ambigram.★ An ambigram that uses a non-Latin alphabet. (This also applies to ambigrams where half of the word is English and the other half is in a different language.)

Perceptual shift. The orientation of this ambigram does not change, but it is read differently depending on how the letters are interpreted.

Miscellaneous. The ambigrams in this category are not encountered as frequently as the others. These could include the following: 3d, containment, web, space-filling, spinonyms, slide, dissection, or word crosses.

★*Some of the multilingual ambigrams in this book require a translation. You will find those in the Credits at the back of the book.*

CHAPTER 3
AMBIGRAM SHOWCASE

Peter/Sarah 180^2
Andy Martin

Jules Verne 180^2
Diego Colombo

America 90^2
David Moser

Pathfinder 180^1
Daniel Dostal

Steampunk
Dan Adona Jr.

 180^1

Reverse Engineering 180^1
Scott Kim

Big
Kirk Visola
 180[1]

Sins
Mark Simonson
180[1]

Allie
Eugene Uymatiao
180[1]

A Lot Of Love
Johan Skylling
 180[1]

Tintin
João Neto
180[1]

Hard Op Wey
Eric Van Den Boom 180^2

Forty Two
Brett J. Gilbert

Pasko!
Dan Adona Jr. 180^1

Mementomori ↰180[1]
Vineeth Nair

China/Japan ↰180[2]
Tiffany Harvey

Courage ↰180[1]
Sam Alfano

Inspiration! ↰180[1]
Robert Maitland

New York
Robert Petrick

Venezia
Alessandro Pocaterra

↑180[1]   **A**|文

True Love
Cheryl Savala

↑180[1]

◄ **Amelie**
Brett J. Gilbert

↑180[1]

◄ **Elite**
Johan Skylling

↑180[1]

Fiona/M'Love
Carl Mehling

Remember 180[1]
Tiffany Harvey

Life/Death 180[2]
Seb Lester

Elite 180[1]
Aditya S. Murthy

Eleventh
Cleber Faria

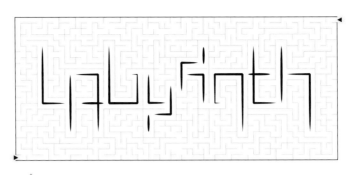

Labyrinth 180[1]
Krzysztof Sliwa

Lovekraft 180[1]
John Langdon

Fizzy 180[1]
Hidden Characters

Enigma 180[1]
Jan Zabransky

Homage 180[1]
Jeff Jenkins

Playhard 180[1]
Charles Madrid

Jump 180[1]
Alexandre Nami Neto

Her Fearful Symmetry 180[1]
NAGFA

Soul of Laos 180²
Basile Morin

Trick or Treat 180²
Elwin Gill

Square/Circle
Jessica Southwick

Paris
Dave Bailey
 180¹

Microeconomics

Microeconomics
Homero Larrain
180¹

Xmatrix
Jeremy Goode
 180¹

Memory
Nabil Harb
 180¹

Hartling
Pit Hartling
 180[1]

Life/Death
Charles Krausie
 180[2]

Revelation
Mark Simonson
 180[1]

Austin/Texas
Nicholas Gilbert

180²

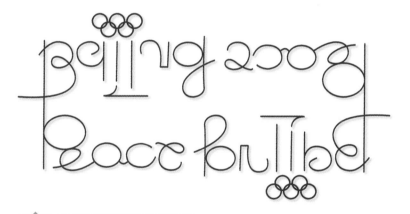

Beijing 2008/Peace for Tibet 180²
Alessandro Pocaterra

Once Upon A Time/Happily Ever After 180²
Mark Hunter

Learning Journey
NAGFA

Mythai
Roberto De Vicq de Cumptich

Happy Holidays
Jennifer Thorne

Flash
Bastian Pinnenberg

Jesus/Christ
Punya Mishra

Spatial/Abstract
Patrice Hamel

Chicago Skyline
Colin Christie

Queen Bee
Tom Banwell

Ringworld **180¹**
Bastian Pinnenberg

Medieval Times **180¹**
Good and Evil Twins

Love You/Forever 180²
Sharath Kumar K.

Cross/word 180²
Patrick Merrell

Black/Gray/White
Robert Maitland

Paradox 180¹
Punya Mishra

Te Amo/Te Odio
Prudencia Hernandez Rodriguez
 180² A|文

Strings
Alejandro Ayala
180¹

Left/Right
Pallavi Karambelkar
 A|A

Mercy/Health
Beth Gully
180²

Manila
Danny J. Cris
180¹

Let it snow
Rebecca May Chabotte

Angels & Demons
Clayton Mabey

Remzi
Temeshi

Faust
Robert Petrick

Reflets de Lettres
Patrice Hamel

Failure/Success
Sharath Kumar K.

Cash/Love
Tiffany Harvey

180^2

Maria
Stefan Vasilev
180^1

Nexus
Tom Banwell

Infinity
Scott Kim

Minister
Suhas Shetty
180[1]

Ektopia
Martin Schmetzer
180[1]

People Power/Martial Law
Dan Adona Jr.
180[2]

Rest In Peace
Nicholas Gilbert
180[2]

Typophile
Mark Simonson
180[1]

Mark and Candice 180^2
Mark Palmer

Aire 180^1 **A**|文
John Moore

Filosofia 180^1 **A**|文
Lisa Nemetz

Honey 180^1
Steve DeCusatis

Triumph 180^1
Prajyot Damle

Angel
Robert Petrick

180^1

Dan Chan The Magic Man 180²
Johan Skylling

Lumiere/Cinematographe 180¹ **A**|文
Daniel Dostal

Calligraphy
Elwin Gill

Erika
Eugene Uymatiao

Corazón
Javier Sanchez Galvan
 **A** | 文

Magic
Prajyot Damle

Sans Serif
Craig Eliason

Rock n Roll
Dave Bailey

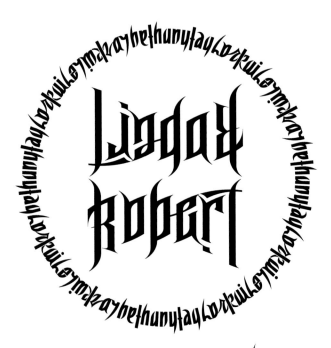

Linda & Robert
Bethany/Taylor/Kailey/McKay
Clayton Mabey

Apollonia
Niels Shoe Meulman
180[1]

Jules Verne
Nabil Harb
180[2]

Tit For Tat
Pallavi Karambelkar
180[2] **A**|文

Steel Driving Man
Colin Christie

Santana
Robert Petrick

Excellence
John Langdon

Smile/Frown
Nicholas Gilbert

Laurel and Hardy
John Moore

Vittoria
John Langdon

Rest In Peace
Mark Hunter

Rock n Roll
Kai Hammond

Coffee
Marcos Mazzei

Reality/Illusion
Sharath Kumar K.

Chirp 180[1]
Todd Weber

Voltica 180[1]
Lisa Nemetz

Daily Planet 180[1]
Daniel Dostal

Fifty 180[1]
Niels Shoe Meulman

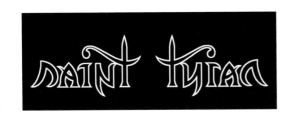

Saint Tyran
Basile Morin

Will Shortz
Patrick Merrell

Friends/Family 180²
Elwin Gill

English?/Français
Patrice Hamel

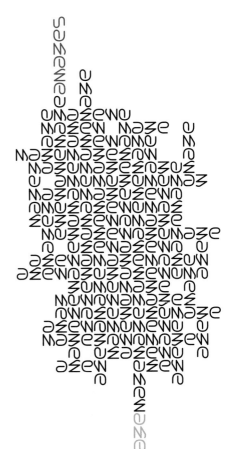

A Maze Amazes
Brett J. Gilbert

Heaven
Johan Skylling ↻ 180[1]

East
David Moser ↻ 90[2] **A**|文

John
Clayton Mabey ↻ 180[1]

Love/Lust
Homero Larrain **A** / **A** ↺

Recycle
Nicholas Gilbert ↻ 180[1]

Labyrinth
Jeremy Goode

↻ 180[1]

Menagerie

Menagerie
Cheryl Savala
180[1]

Brahms

Brahms
Scott Kim
180[1]

Jackson
Tiffany Harvey
180[1]

Jungletales
Uttam Sikaria
180[1]

Number 25
Tom Banwell

White Rabbit

White Rabbit
Homero Larrain
180[1]

Denim With Attitude
Mark Palmer

↰180²

Symphonie
Eutimos Paramatatya

↰180¹ **A**|文

Cheap
Hidden Characters

↰180¹

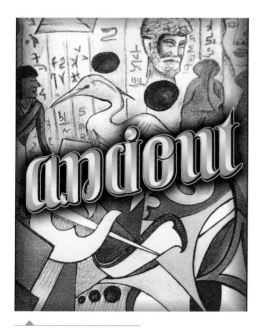

Ancient/Modern
Sharath Kumar K.

↰180²

Hephaestus
Sam Alfano
 180[1]

Elvis
Vasileios Stergioudis

 A | A

Monica
Javier Sanchez Galvan
 180[1]

DJ Shadow
Tom Bogman
 180[1]

Yoga
Anna Kupstova 180[1]

Drink/Drunk
Mark Simonson 180[2]

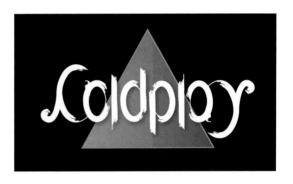

Coldplay
Vineeth Nair

180[1]

Happy Holidays
René Oswaldo González Pizarro 180[2]

Wilfred/Cynthia
Rebecca May Chabotte 180[2]

Lancelot
Jessica Southwick
↻180[1]

Googly
Uttam Sikaria
↻180[1]

Shoe/Patta
*Niels Shoe
Meulman*
↻180[2] A|文

Faith
Beth Weiss
↻180[1]

Jennifer
Eugene Uymatiao
↻180[1]

Rammer
*Rammer Martínez
Sánchez*
↻180[1]

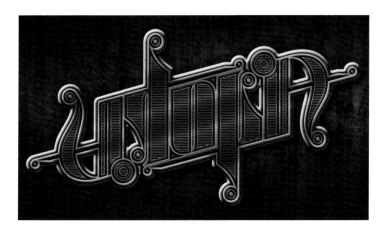

Great Britain
Robert Maitland

180[1]

Utopia
Tim Costello

180[1]

Sea
David Moser

90[2] $\mathbf{A}$|文

Hell
Johan Skylling

180[1]

Moscow
Andrey Kruglov

180[1]

MOSCOW

Louis Armstrong
John Langdon

Links
Punya Mishra

Asterisk
Robert Maitland 180[1]

Family/Friends
Tiffany Harvey 180[2]

M.C. Escher
Scott Kim

Tokyo
David Moser

Love/Fuck
Seb Lester

The Blue Man Group
Martijn Slegers ⤾180¹

Leonardo da Vinci
Daniel Dostal

⤾180¹

London 2012
Chirag Gander

Dig In ▶
Carl Mehling

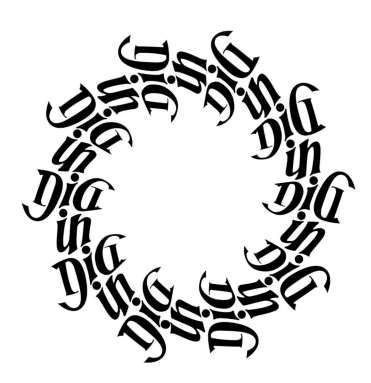

Ian and Tristan ▶
Bastian Pinnenberg

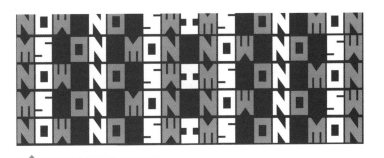

Now No Swims On Mon 180[1]
Nick Sahli

Perfect 180[1]
Alejandro Ayala

Sex Drugs & Rock n Roll 180[2]
Awang Purba

Life & Death 180[2]
John Langdon

Coffee
Patrick Merrell

Elena
Stefan Vasilev

Ravel
Scott Kim

Papercut
Johan Skylling

True Love
Dave Bailey

Love Never Dies 180^2
Daniel Dostal

Innovate
Charles Madrid

180^1

TOP TEN TIPS FOR CREATING AMBIGRAMS

Creating ambigrams is such a flexible art form that it's difficult to narrow down exact steps. And the more you read about ambigrammists and their styles, the more you'll realize that each ambigram is unique and that the design process is very personal for each designer. You too will need to develop, define, and refine your own process. However, the following ten tips from the pros will help you get started.

1. **Choices, choices.** The success of your ambigram begins with word choice and letter-form analysis. Keep in mind that not every word can become a good ambigram.

2. **Research.** Before you start creating ambigrams, learn about graphic design, typography, and color. Go to libraries and old bookstores to search for visual inspiration. Visit museums and art galleries. Use various online resources, some of which you will find on the next page. And, of course, research ambigrams to see what has and hasn't been done.

3. **Simplicity is key.** At first, learn how to make a legible and readable ambigram from simple words. Then apply various typographic styles to it so you can learn how they affect the legibility of your ambigram. As your skills improve, progress to more complex words.

4. **Sketch, sketch, and sketch some more.** If you want to create a truly unique ambigram, paper and pencil should be your starting point. Experimenting with different letter combinations and ratios on paper is the only way to account for all possibilities.

5. **Function first, style second.** The style of the ambigram manifests itself throughout the development process and should never be set in stone beforehand. When you base your ambigram on an existing style from the beginning (be it a certain typography style or even an existing typeface), you trap yourself in a corner if the chosen word requires extensive letter manipulation.

6. **Consistency.** Use a consistent lettering style, letter spacing, and letter heights to achieve readability. Strive to find letter shapes that are clear and unambiguous. If a particular letter shape just isn't working, consider using an alternate form of the letter.

7. **Don't be predictable.** If your ambigram contains predictable letter combinations, take the time to explore other solutions. Context is important, so explore various letter combinations with respect to their location within the word. Even if a certain combination may not work within one word, it may work in a future ambigram. Some letter flips are unavoidable, whereas others offer a lot of flexibility.

8. **Colors, textures, and flourishes—oh my!** Only after your design works in black and white should you consider adding color, outlines, shading, and other graphic embellishments.

9. **Take your time.** Spend a lot of time on research and sketching. Don't be in a hurry to jump on the computer to digitize your work because that is probably the last 5 percent of the process. The initial 95 percent of the ambigram design process is research, sketching, and exploration.

10. **What does that ambigram say?** You already know what your ambigram says, so you are not the best judge of its legibility. Show your ambigram to other people to see if they can read it.

RESOURCES

This resources list contains information relevant to ambigrams, typography, lettering, and graphic design. At the time of the development and publication of this book, all the resource URLs were functional.

RESEARCH

- **www.ambigramsrevealed.com.** This is the companion website for *Ambigrams Revealed*. You will be able to find submission samples and ambigram-related quotes from the participants.

- **www.ambigram.com.** Ambigram.com is the biggest online community for ambigram-mists and ambigram admirers. Here you can find interviews with artists, ambigram challenges, and other ambigram information.

- **tdc.org.** The Type Directors Club is an international organization that focuses on print and digital typography.

- **www.howdesign.com.** *HOW* magazine is one of the premiere graphic design magazines in the world.

- **www.cmykmag.com.** *CMYK* is a design magazine that showcases diverse design work ranging from students to professional designers and design firms.

- **www.typophile.com.** Typophile is a free forum that promotes discussions on anything and everything typography related.

- **ilovetypography.com.** I Love Typography is the brain child of John Boardley who is a British-born designer living in Vietnam. In his own words, "This site aims to make the subject more accessible and to bring the study of typography to the masses."

- **www.lettercult.com.** LetterCult showcases amazing custom-lettering work from designers around the world.

- **typedia.com.** Typedia is an online community dedicated to the classification of type-faces, as well as educating people about typography.

- **www.dailytype.ru.** Daily Type is curated by several Russian type designers. They focus on the creation of original typefaces, as well as the process behind it.

- **www.typographyserved.com.** Typography Served features top work in categories such as typeface design, lettering, illustrated typography, or any piece with a strong typographic treatment. It is is a Behance served website: Behance is the leading online platform to show-case and discover creative work.

- **www.typographica.org.** Typographica is a website that reviews typefaces and type books.

SOFTWARE

- **Inkscape.org.** Inkscape is a free, downloadable, vector drawing program available for Mac and Windows. It has similar capabilites to Adobe Illustrator, CorelDraw, and Freehand.

- **Lynda.com.** This website contains video-based software tutorials for various software programs, including Illustrator, Photoshop, and CorelDraw.

CREDITS

Adona Jr., Dan. Phillipines. Pasko (p116), steampunk (p114), peoplepower/martiallaw (p132). Designed by Dan Adona Jr., imagefoundry@yahoo.com, imagefoundry.wordpress.com.

Alfano, Sam. United States. Courage (p117), hephaestus (p114). Designed by Sam Alfano. ©2012 Sam Alfano - Masterengraver.com.

Ayala, Alejandro. Venezuela. perfect (p151), strings (p129). Designed by Alejandro Ayala.

Bailey, Dave. United States. Paris (p123), rock n roll (p135), truelove (p153). Designed by Dave Bailey, ©2012.

Banwell, Tom. United States. Nexus (p131), queen bee (p127), number 25 (p142), shark attack (p68). Designed by Tom Banwell.

Bogman, Tom. The Netherlands. Dj Shadow (p144). Designed by By Tom Bogman.

Christie, Colin. United States. Steel Driving Man (p137), Chicago Skyline (p127). Designed by Colin Christie.

Chabotte, Rebecca M. United States. Let it snow (p130), wilfred/cynthia (p145). Designed by Rebecca May, d.b.a. Ambigram Greetings.

Colombo, Diego. Italy. Jules Verne (p114). Designed by Arch. Diego Colombo, drdiegocolombo@gmail.com.

Costello, Tim. Japan. Utopia (p147). Designed by Tim Costello.

Cris, Danny J. Philippines. Manila (p129). Designed by Danny J. Cris, dannyjcris@engineer.com.

de Cumptich, Roberto De Vicq. United States. Mythai (p126). Designed by Roberto De Vicq de Cumptich/ de Vicq design.

Damle, Prajyot. India. Magic (p135), triumph (p133). Designed by Prajyot Damle, prajyot-ambigrams.blogspot.com.

DeCusatis, Steve. United States. Honey (p133). Designed by Steve DeCusatis Design, stevedecusatis.com, stevedecusatis.com/blog.

Dieterich, Mark. neptune yachts (p14)

Dostal, Daniel. Poland. Pathfinder (p11), love never dies (p153), dailyplanet (p138), leonardo davinci (p149), lumiere/cinematographe (p134), wishmaster (case study, p60). Designed by Daniel Dostal, signum et imago http://daneel75.wordpress.com.

Eliason, Craig. United States. Sans serif (p135). Designed by Craig Eliason, Teeline Fonts.

Faria, Cleber. Brasil. Eleventh (p119), history (case study, p57). Designed by Cleber Faria (Duartina/SP - Brasil), www.cleberfaria.com.

Galvan, Javier Sanchez. Mexico. Monica (p114), corazon (p135). Designed by Javier Sánchez, genio + figura, www.genioyfigura.mx.

Gander, Chirag. India. London 2012 (p150). Designed by Chirag Gander, Chittorgarh (Rajasthan), www.facebook.com/Karismatic.Kraft.

Gilbert, Brett J. United Kingdom. Amelie (p118), forty two, (p116) a maze amazes (p140). Designed by Brett J. Gilbert.

Gilbert, Nicholas. United States. Austin/texas (p125), recycle (p141), rest in peace (p132), smile/frown (p138) clean/dirty (case study, p72). Designed by Nicholas Gilbert.

Gill, Elwin. United States. Trick or treat (p122), friends/family (p140), calligraphy (p135), San Diego (case study, p64). Designed by Elwin Gill, www.elwin-gill.com, http://elwingill.wordpress.com.

Good and Evil Twins. Medieval Times (p127). Designed by Good and Evil Twins (Damian Lakey, Joshua Lakey, Mandala Lakey), goodandeviltwins.com.

Goode, Jeremy. United Kingdom. Labyrinth (p141), xmatrix (p123). Designed by Jeremy Goode. Trademark/ Registered ©2012.

Gully, Beth. United States. Mercy/health (p129). Designed by Beth Gully - AniMotionLogos.

Hamel, Patrice. France. Spatial/Abstrait (p126. Translation: Spatial/Abstract. RÉPLIQUE N°42, Version n°1, 2010. Photography: Romain Nicoleau). Reflets de Lettres (p130. Translation: Reflection of Letters. RÉPLIQUE N°2, Version n°3, 2009, Photography: Patrice Hamel.) English?/Français (p140. Translation: Anglais?/French. RÉPLIQUE N°8, Version n°1, 1998. Photography: Patrice Hamel) Designed by Patrice Hamel. ©Patrice Hamel.

Hammond, Kai. United Kingdom. Rock n roll (p138), alphabet (case study, p108). Designed by Kai Hammond, www.cargocollective.com/kaimonington, www.coroflot.com/kaimonington.

Harb, Nabil. Germany. Memory (p123), Jules Verne (p136). Designed by Nabil Harb, n.harb@arcor.de, www.flickr.com/wortgewandt13.

Hartling, Pit. Germany. Hartling (p124). "Pit Hartling" Ambigram Playing Cards. Ambigram created by Pit Hartling, Frankfurt am Main. www.pithartling.com. Playing cards back design, Ace of Spades and card case design by Jorg Willich, Hamburg. www.joergwillich.de.

Harvey, Tiffany. United States. Remember (p119), jackson (p142), cash/love (p131), china/japan (p117), family/friends (p148). Designed by Tiffany Harvey, wordillusion.com.

Hidden Characters. Hungary. Cheap (p143), fizzy (p120). Designed by Hidden Characters, www.hiddencharacters.hu.

Hofstadter, Douglas. Light Is A Wave Particle (p30). Designed by Douglas Hofstadter.

Hunter, Mark. United States. Rest in peace (p138), once upon a time/happily ever after (p125). Designed by Mark Hunter, FlipScript.com.

Jenkins, Jeff. United States. Homage (p120). Designed by Jeff Jenkins.

K, Sharath Kumar. India. Ancient/modern (p143), failure/success (p131), reality/illusion (p139), loveyou/forever (p128). Designed by Sharath Kumar K.

Karambelkar, Pallavi (Apte). India. Tit for tat/टिट फॉर टैट (p136), left/right (p129). Designed by Pallavi (Apte) Karambelkar.

Kim, Scott. United States. Brahms (p142), M.C. Escher (p148), infinity chain (p28), reverse engineering (p114), Ravel (p152), Figure/figure (p24), figure/figure tessellation (p24), Karen (p25), Michael (p25), Inversions/ScottKim (p26), Annie (p24), information (p30), perception/illusion (p31), Hayashi (p31), Schönberg symbol system (p32), Berrocal (p33), John Maeda (p34), ambigram (p29), ohio (p30), Martin Gardner Celebration of the mind/physics patterns and prestidigitation (p34), Martin Gardner Celeberation of the mind/magic mathematics and mystery united (p34). Designed by Scott Kim, www.scottkim.com.

Kowalczyk, Tomasz J. "Temeshi." Poland. Remzi (p130). Designed by Temeshi, www.inmytype.com.

Krausie, Charles. United States. Life/death (p124). Designed by Charles Krausie, San Francisco, CA.

Kruglov, Andrey. Russia. Moscow (p147). Designed by Andrey Kruglov, www.motiondesign.ru.

Kuptsova, Anna. Russia. Yoga (p145). Designed by Anna Kuptsova, www.behance.net/Anlee.

Langdon, John. United States. "Illuminati Diamond" (Earth Air Fire Water. p20), Excellence (p137), Life & Death (p151), Louis Armstrong (p148), Lovekraft (p120), Vittoria (p138), Guthrie (p22), Logo design for Elizabeth Ann Stallone, (p14), Hell/77, (p34), Thursday (p15), Victoria (p16), Starship (p16), Philosophy (p17), Wordplay (p18), Angels & Demons (p19), Guthrie (p21), Chain Reaction (p37). Designed by John Langdon, www.johnlangdon.net.

Larrain, Homero. Chile. Microeconomics (p123), white rabbit (p142), love/lust (p141). Designed by Homero Larrain.

Lester, Seb. United Kingdom. Love/fuck (p149), life/death (p119), sunshine blazing (case study, p80). Designed by Seb Lester, www.seblester.co.uk.

Mabey, Clayton. United States. John (p141), angels & demons (p130), Linda&/Robert(Bethany, Taylor, Kailey, McKay) (p136), John Langdon + Scott Kim (case study, p92). Designed by Clayton Mabey, customambigrams.com.

Madrid, Charles Omar. Philippines. Innovate (p153), playhard (p121). Designed by Charles Omar Madrid, charlesambigram.blogspot.com.

Maitland, Robert. Canada. Inspiration (p117), black/gray/white (p128), GreatBritain (p147), asterisk (p148). Designed by Robert Maitland. ©Robert Maitland. Ambigramdesign.wordpress.com.

Martin, Andy. United Kingdom. Peter/Sarah (p114). Designed by Andy Martin.

Mazzei, Marcos. Brasil. Coffee (p138). Designed by Marcos Mazzei. Calligraphy Pen - square nib.

Mehling, Carl. United States. Dig in (p150), Fiona/m'love (p119), tempt (case study, p76). Designed by Carl Mehling.

Merrell, Patrick. United States. Cross/word (p128), coffee (p152), Will Shortz (p140). Designed by Patrick Merrell. ©Patrick Merrell.

Meulman, Niels Shoe. The Netherlands. Apollonia (p136), fifty (p139), shoe/patta (*patta* is the Surinamese word for shoe, p146). Designed by Niels Shoe Meulman, www.nielsshoemeulman.com.

Mishra, Punya. United States. Jesus Christ (p126), links (p148), paradox (p128). Designed by Punya Mishra, punyamishra.com.

Moore, John. Venezuela. Aire (p133, Translation: air.), Laurel/Hardy (p138). Designed by John J.Moore, www.johnmoore.com.ve.

Morin, Basile. France. Saint/tyran (p140), Soul of Laos (p122). Designed by Basile Morin, www.ambigramme.com.

Moser, David. China. Tokyo (p149. Horizontally the graph reads "TOKYO," and turned 90-degrees counterclockwise, it reads 東京, the word for "China" in both Japanese Kanji and Chinese traditional characters, as used in Taiwan and Hong Kong). Sea (p147. This reads "SEA" horizontally in English. Turned clockwise, the character is 海, "ocean/sea" in both Japanese and Chinese). America (p114. The horizontal reading is "AMERICA," and turned clockwise the Chinese translation, 美国). East (p141. This reads EAST horizontally, turned counterclockwise the character 東 "East" in both Chinese and Japanese). Designed by David Moser.

Murthy, Aditya S. India. Elite (p119). Designed by Aditya S. Murthy, adityasm9@gmail.com.

NAGFA. Singapore. Her fearful symmetry (p121), learning journey (p126), kingfisher (case study, p88). Designed by NAGFA (Mohamed Naguib bin Ngadnan & Fadilah bte Abdul Rahim).

Nair, Vineeth G. India. Coldplay (p145), mementomori (p117). Designed by Dr. Vineeth G. Nair. http://why-so-symmetrical.blogspot.in.

Nemetz, Lisa. Argentina. Filosofia (p133), Voltica (p139). "Voltica - Ambigram Typeface" Designed by Lisa Nemetz, www.lisanemetz.com.

Neto, Alexandre Nami. Brasil. Jump (p121). Designed by Alexandre Nami.

Neto, João. Portugal. Tintin (p115). Designed by João Neto.

Nicolas, Alain. Tessellation (p33). Parcellesdinfini.free.fr. Parcelles d'infini. ©Editions Pour la Science 2005.

Palmer, Mark. United States. Denim with attitude (p143), Mark/Candice (p133), shark attack (case study, p68). Designed by Mark Palmer, founder/ambigram artist at RedChapterClothing.com and Wowtattoos.com.

Paramatatya, Eutimos. Indonesia. Symphonie (p143). Designed by Eutimos Paramatatya, ©2012.

Pizarro, René Oswaldo González. Mexico. Happy holidays (p145). Designed by René Oswaldo González Pizarro (aka Serpiente).

Petrick, Robert. United States. Angel (p133), New York (p117), Santana (p137), Faust (p130). Designed by Robert W. Petrick. www.robertpetrick.com/angel1976.html, www.robertpetrick.com/rwponline.html, www.robertpetrick.com.

Pinnenberg, Bastian. Germany. Flash (p126), Ian and Tristan (p150), ringworld (p127), snapstar (case study, p100). Designed by Bastian Pinnenberg.

Pocaterra, Alessandro. Italy. Beijing 2008/Peace for Tibet (p125), Venezia (p118). Designed by Alessandro Pocaterra.

Prokhorov, Nikita. United States. Eureka (p2), Sins (p4), Chump (p4), Emilio (p6), Italia (p9), Klimt (p9), Elizabeth (p14). Designed by Nikita Prokhorov, www.elusiveillusion.com.

Purba, Awang. Malaysia. Sex, Drugs & Rock n Roll (p151). Designed by Awang Purba.

Rodriguez, Prudencia Hernandez. Mexico. Te amo/te odio (p129. Translation: I hate you/I love you). Designed by Pru HRdz/genio + figura, www.genioyfigura.mx.

Sahli, Nick. United States. Nownoswimsonmon (p151). Designed by Nick Sahli.

Sánchez, Rammer Martínez. United States. Rammer (p146). Designed by Rammer Martínez Sánchez, smokymirrors.com.

Savala, Cheryl. United States. Menagerie (p142), true love (p118). Designed by Cheryl Savala. ©2013 Menagerie Creative, Inc.

Schmetzer, Martin. Sweden. Ektopia (p132). Designed by Martin Schmetzer, martinschmetzer.com.

Simonson, Mark. United States. Typophile (p132), revelation (p124), sins (p115), drink/drunk (p145).Designed by Mark Simonson, www.marksimonson.com.

Shetty, Suhas, United States. Minister (p132). Designed by Suhas Shetty.

Sikaria, Uttam. India. Googly (p146), jungletales (p142. Translation: It reads "JungleTales." "Jungle" is written in devanagri as जंगल, which means the same as "Jungle" in English. "Tales" is the English word. JungleTales is the title of Annual Magazine for Hostel 8, IIT Bombay. In exact literals, the ambigram reads जंगल**tales**.

Slegers, Martijn. The Netherlands. The Blue Man Group (p149), Mystery Gift (case study, p84). Designed by Martijn Slegers, martijnslegers.blogspot.nl.

Sliwa, Krzysztof. Poland. Labyrinth (p120). Designed by Krzysztof Sliwa.

Stergioudis, Vasileios. Greece. Elvis (p144). Designed by Vasileios Stergioudis.

Skylling, Johan. Sweden. A lot of love (p115), Dan Chan the magic man (p134), elite (p118), hell (p147), papercut (p152). Designed by Johan "Sparris" Skylling.

Southwick, Jessica. United States. Lancelot (p14), Square/circle (p122). Designed by Jessica Southwick – Jesswick Creative Studio, LLC.

Thorne, Jennifer. United States. Happy holidays (p126). Designed by Jennifer Thorne, www.imriaylde.com.

Uymatiao, Eugene. Australia. Erika (p135), Allie (p115), Jennifer (p146), turn of phrase (p107, The King of Diamonds, The Queen of Diamonds, The Jack of Diamonds, The Ace of Diamonds, King of Clubs, and Ace of Hearts).

Vasilev, Stefan. Bulgaria. Elena (p152), Maria (p131). Designed by Stefan Vasilev, www.dreamerworx.com.

Van Den Boom, Eric. The Netherlands. Hard op wey (p116). Designed by BoomArtwork, www.boomartwork.com

Visola, Kirk. United States. Big (p115). Designed by Kirk Visola, www.kirkvisola.com.

Weber, Todd. United States. Chirp (p139). Designed by Todd Weber, A Studio Called Chirp.

Weiss, Elizabeth A. United States. Faith (p146). Designed by Beth Weiss.

Winklepleck, Jen. United States. Unseen (case study, p96). Designed by Jen Winklepleck, www.jensaysdotcom.net.

Zabransky, Jan. Czech Republic. Enigma (p120). Designed by Jan Zabransky.

xpedx logo and the photograph of the xpedx truck (p4). xpedx and the xpedx logo are registered trademarks of International Paper and are used with permission. xpedx is the distribution business of International Paper.

Photo of Nikita Prokhorov (p2) by Corey Lynn Tucker Photography. www.facebook.com/coreylynntucker.